POSITIVE LIVING

THROUGH INNER HEALING

H.J. Vander Molen
Christmas 1978

POSITIVE LIVING THROUGH INNER HEALING

by Genevieve Parkhurst

LOGOS INTERNATIONAL
Plainfield, New Jersey

Positive Living Through Inner Healing

Published 1978 by Logos International
Printed in the United States of America
International Standard Book Number: 0-88270-283-1
Library of Congress Catalog Card Number: 78-60767

Originally entitled *Glorious Victory Through Healing The Memories*

DEDICATION

This book is dedicated to ministers and friends I have known in their youth, in various churches and in Northwestern College, Alva, Oklahoma.

ACKNOWLEDGEMENT

So many people have contributed to the content of this book that it is impossible to name them all, for each person with whom I have counseled during the past years, has helped me to understand the needs of persons who suffer from hidden hurts, repressed since childhood. I am especially grateful to the friends who have allowed the stories of their experience to be included in this book. I deeply appreciate the helpfulness of my husband, George A. Parkhurst, and of our son, George E. Parkhurst M.D., Psychiatrist, without whose help this book could not have been written.

Genevieve Parkhurst

AUTHOR'S PREFACE

After writing and discarding numerous efforts to compose a fitting preface for this book, I find I can say nothing as apropos as does Fritz Kunkel, medical doctor and psychologist whose work was well known on both sides of the Atlantic. Dr. Kunkel had no interest in Christianity, but one day he picked up the New Testament to see what the man Jesus had to say in the light of modern psychology. To his amazement, he discovered that Jesus was the greatest psychologist of all time, that he asked the right questions and always gave the right answers. Dr. Kunkel not only found Jesus, the great psychologist, but he found Jesus, the Savior. As a result Dr. Kunkel lectured and wrote a number of books in his effort to establish a firm foundation between modern psychology and the teachings of Jesus. I am grateful for the permission to let his words be the preface to this book.

"The newest branches which emerged out of the unfolding tree of science, namely psychology and sociology, were almost unaware of the fact that religion and theology had handled the human soul and human society for countless centuries. The prophets of the Old Testament were practical sociologists. Jesus of Nazareth was the greatest psychologist of all times. But the riches of tradition, accumulated in religious literature and art, were neglected, and theology made no attempt to fight. It gave in, ignoring for many years the new sciences as they in turn ignored theology. Later, however, the ministers began to realize that they needed more knowledge of the human mind, as well as of social relations. So they began to study the secular psychology and sociology as they found them — instead of creating their own Christian sociology and psychology and teaching their secular colleagues the deeper truth and the stronger power that was entrusted to Christianity from the beginning.

"There was growing social suffering, and a pagan like Karl Marx had to appear — and work out a wrong way of salvation; there was increasing individual suffering, and again a pagan like Sigmund Freud had to appear to show a wrong way of salvation. Why did not the Christian Church, the guardian of the human soul and social relationships, produce another Amos, Saint Paul, or Augustine to show the way out? Theology could withdraw from natural science, philosophy, and even art; but to surrender the fields of psychology and sociology was a strategic error that almost sealed the universal defeat of Christianity.

"We must make up for this mistake, or Christianity will die out. The human mind is the central domain of religious life. We should not claim that we are the only experts who understand this field and are allowed to work in it; we should be grateful if other experts from different viewpoints share in our research; but we should be able to demonstrate that Christians know more about human life, human personality and human society than their secular fellow-research men. It should be a free and fair competition in which the spiritual power of Christianity could show its creativeness. We should admire all the great sociologists and psychologists, learn from them, but do better than they. If the Christian viewpoint is true, then it must lead both to theoretical knowledge and to practical findings. It cannot remain other-worldly. If it is true, it has to work in practical life and validate itself."[1]

Genevieve Parkhurst

---

[1]In Search of Maturity, by Fritz Kunkel M.D. Charles Scribner's Sons. N.Y. pages 12 and 13. Used by permission.

TABLE OF CONTENTS

FOREWORD

Among present day writers Genevieve Parkhurst stands out as one who is able to perceive below the superficial surface of ordinary life, and to see what makes man tick. For the third time she has written a book which pierces through religiosity, intellectualism, through the trivia of life into the area where Christ's teachings are relevant to everyday living. She has been able in this book to dramatically present a few of man's problems and to make clear their solution. In doing so, she bridges walls or compartments, which for centuries have separated religion from science, religion from psychology, and the natural from the supernatural, thus bringing to us a better view of the whole of God's grace and of man's beliefs and unbeliefs.

With the present day knowledge explosion, it is difficult for an individual to grasp that which is presented in more than one field. It seems necessary to compartmentalize and separate one area of knowledge from another. Many persons can cry out that something is wrong but few are able to point out the cure. Here is an author who fuses the psychological with the supernatural of the spiritual in a smoothe and orderly way that makes sense.

Being a psychiatrist and having received training to

believe only what one can see, feel, measure, or test in some way, I wonder if religious teachers have not also taught their students to accept from the Bible only that which can be accepted by reason, and to disregard the miraculous. In doing this their student seminarians are being brain-washed to a sterile religion.

Today more and more ministers are being trained in counselling. Ministers usually deal with emotional problems of their parishioners in one of three ways. First: They may ignore them. Second: They may pray that God will intervene. Third: They may counsel without prayer, relying on psychological techniques. This book presents a counselling-prayer combination which should enable ministers to give valuable help to their parishioners who come to them seeking help. It affords a new look into the area of pastoral counselling for the minister's consideration.

George E. Parkhurst M.D.
Tulsa, Oklahoma

1

We Seek a Satisfying Life

> BUT THANKS BE TO GOD, WHO IN CHRIST ALWAYS LEADS US IN TRIUMPH, AND THROUGH US SPREADS THE FRAGRANCE OF THE KNOWLEDGE OF HIM EVERYWHERE.
>
> II Corinthians 2:14 (R.S.V.)

A stir of expectancy rippled over the congregation as the young minister rose to speak. For a moment he seemed tense. But now, he faced his audience calm and poised. A handsome young man of athletic build, he seemed to possess every quality of leadership. He began his sermon with a story apropos to his theme and told it well. But as he approached the body of his sermon he hesitated uncertainly. He had chosen a great theme, a great text. Would he proclaim it with the power of a firm conviction?

No. He wavered as if undecided as to what grounds to take on a subject that might be controversial. He seemed to be debating. But with whom? With himself?

I glanced at the people around me. Had they caught this note of uncertainty? I hoped not, for I was jealous for this young man's success. Listening to him was like hearing my own son speak.

These two had been inseparable during their grade

school years. The Houstons who were friends had lived near us. As I watched Stanley Houston now I felt as if I were his mother, unable to move, while he struggled in deep water.

At the close of the service he stood at the front door, with words of greeting for each one, shaking hands as they left the sanctuary. I smiled as I went out but hurried on my way.

My husband was preaching for a neighboring pastor who was on vacation, so I was alone this morning. I was almost home when I remembered I had put some notes in the hymnal I had used, so I drove back to the church to get them.

The lights were out in the sanctuary and it seemed vacant. But as I walked down the aisle I saw a figure slumped in a seat, his arms on the back of the pew in front of him and his head resting on his hands. Quietly I slipped past him, got my paper and started out again. The slumped figure raised his head as I neared him.

It was Stanley.

"I'm sorry," he said, "I'm very tired."

"Try to take things easier," I offered, then added, "you may be working too hard."

As I stood in the darkened foyer, a door to the rostrum opened and Lee Masters, Educational Director of the church, walked in. He went back of the pulpit where he stood looking over the sanctuary. For some moments he stood there smiling, then he shrugged his shoulders and walked out.

After Lee had gone Stan rose and left by the front door, unmindful that I stood in the shadows. There might have been more here than met the eye. Could this little drama hold the key to Stanley's exhaustion, I wondered as I drove home?

The work of the ministry is demanding, I know since

I have spent most of my life in Methodist Parsonages. A minister may be expected to preach like Saint Paul, be a juggler who is able to keep all organizations of his church in motion simultaneously, be expected to call every member of his congregation by name, visit all newcomers of his faith as soon as they move to town and visit all who are sick and shut-in. He should be a man among men, a gracious gentleman among ladies, the life of the party when with young people. He must comfort the bereaved, encourage the distressed, laugh with those who laugh and be a sparkling conversationalist at every dinner table. While all of these things may be expected of him, a minister's main duty is to lead his people into fellowship with God. This requires his best effort and tension among his church staff undermines a minister's energy.

Was Lee Masters a thorn in Stan's flesh? Lee was a friend of our former pastor who had brought him to this church. They had gotten along well, but was Masters now trying to take church matters into his own hands? Was he unwilling to accept the leadership of another?

George and I were delighted when Stanley Houston was appointed to a suburban church in our city. As soon as he and his wife arrived, they had come to our home for dinner.

Stanley felt at home at once and proudly introduced Elizabeth. Her outward appearance left nothing to be desired. She moved gracefully, her blue eyes sparkled as she smiled and her glowing natural complexion denoted radiant health. Warmly she clasped my extended hand saying, in a voice low and musical, "Stan has talked so much about you. I feel that I know you already. I hope I may call you Aunt Gen."

Memories, awhile forgotten, arose to transport us back into the yesterdays. Stan recalled boyhood pranks involving himself and our son. He briefed Beth on these stories and as we laughed she laughed with us. The food reminded Stan of other meals eaten from these dishes and by the time the evening was over happiness filled the house so that our guests seemed reluctant to leave.

"It is like having one of our children home," George said as he turned off the porch light. "Stan has developed into a splendid young man. Really, he seems to have every requisite for a successful pastor. He should make a success of his ministry."

"Indeed he does," I agreed. "He has looks and brains, poise and graciousness, and with such a wife as Beth, there seems to be nothing to stop his progress in his work in the Church."

Now, as I drove from church, I felt concerned for Stanley, but I would not interfere. I certainly was not parading the fact that I knew him when — or telling stories of his boyhood which might embarass this aspiring young minister. He knew where George and I lived if he wanted to see us.

During services on following Sundays the tension I had felt seemed to be manifest by a feeling of haste, as if it was necessary to get the service over as soon as possible. Was there an electric current between the tall man, Houston, in the pulpit and the slightly built Masters, tenor soloist in the choir?

One evening at dinner I voiced by misgivings about Stan's relationship with the Educational Director of the church.

"Oh, no!" George exclaimed. "Don't tell me he is having trouble getting along with the young men as well as with the older ones."

"Now what?" I looked up questioningly.

"I didn't intend to mention this," George shook his head sadly. "I was hoping there was nothing to the flair up that occurred in the last board meeting, but since you have brought up this other incident, I am afraid they tie together."

"What happened."

"Well, you know Dan Lathum. He always is in disagreement with the majority. He can put things over when they are his ideas but when opposed, he can be as stubborn as a mule and about as discourteous. During the meeting, Stanley made some suggestions, Dan opposed him, Stan tried to explain his position and Dan jumped all over him. Stan became so angry his face got flaming red, veins in his neck stood out and he seemed to exert great effort to keep his composure. It really was quite unreasonable for a young man in his position to become so unnerved. When he tried to speak his voice was hoarse and strained."

"Oh, don't tell me that," I cried, dropping my head in my hands.

"The boy has everything in his favor," George went on. "It must be the deep resentment he felt toward his father that flares up when an older man acts toward him as his father used to. He never can make a success in the ministry so long as he carries this sore spot around to throw him into childhood anger every time he is rubbed the wrong way. Above all things, a minister must be able to get along with people. He must like people, not just pretend to."

"I am so sorry to know this," I said.

After a moment George went on, "It really seems strange that a minister, with his calling and training, should retain hurts that would influence his actions."

"Neither the good nor the strong are immune from traumatic memories," I said. "Most often it is the sensitive and those who have clear memory recall who suffer most from abuse. These may be persons who are efficient and highly endowed mentally. Having known Stan's father can you wonder that the boy carries scars from his treatment."

"You may be able to help Stan," George added. "I hope you can, he certainly needs it."

2

The Reach of the Mind

O LORD, THOU HAST SEARCHED ME, AND KNOWN ME. THOU KNOWEST MY DOWNSITTING AND MY UPRISING, THOU UNDERSTANDETH MY THOUGHT AFAR OFF. THOU COMPASSEST MY PATH AND MY LYING DOWN, AND ART ACQUAINTED WITH ALL MY WAYS. FOR THERE IS NOT A WORD IN MY TONGUE, BUT, LO, O LORD, THOU KNOWEST IT ALTOGETHER.

Psalm 138:1-4 (KJ)

A few days later, when George had left for the country after an early lunch and I was working in my study, Stan telephoned asking if he might come by for a few minutes.

"Do come, Stan," I answered happily, "I shall be glad to see you."

The front door was open to the balmy spring breeze and soon a cheery voice called, "Hello, is anybody home?"

"Come in Stan, I'll be right with you," I answered.

"Let me come where you are," he said, striding through the living room to my workshop. Vibrant with health and eyes twinkling with good humor, Stan swung around the room. "I hurried from the office before anyone could catch me. This weather makes me want to play hookie," he grinned.

"I feel the same way but I did want to finish this chapter," I said.

"I'll bet Uncle George is doing what he wants to do and is out at his ranch right now."

"Yes, the air out there has a sort of exhilaration."

"I think he's got it made," Stan mused. "to have completed a successful ministry, and now to have horses and white faced cattle to ride among. That's the life."

"Sit down," I suggested. But Stan came to my desk and picking up a paper scanned it quickly.

"What's this? Are you writing another book?"

"I'm working at it."

"What is it about?"

Pushing papers from me, I turned from my desk, "It is about healing the memories." I said, watching Stan's face.

"About what?"

"Releasing hurts and resentments which can warp our lives, so that association with them shall not hinder our actions as we face circumstances of like nature during our present activities."

"Stan squinted one eye and looked at me quizzically. "You really think that can be done?"

"Oh yes, it is quite possible." I answered.

Pursing his lips, Stan stood a moment in thought, then offered, "I suppose psychiatrists do this sort of thing, but you — pardon me, Aunt Gen — but how could you do such a thing? Your work is in the field of prayer, as I understand it."

"You are right, I don't do it. I only guide the person in need of such help to the One who is able to do it for him. I help him to make contact with the Divine Mind which is able to enter into our human minds and help us to release memories of hurtful experiences that are there."

"Heavens! who needs to be shown that such hurts are there?" Stan exclaimed. "What we need is to get rid of them."

"Yes," I agreed, "and that is the next step in the Holy Spirit's action."

"You're kidding," Stan smiled. "It may be that God can forgive man's sins, but to go into his memory and take out the hurts from traumatic experiences, that is too much. Please, Aunt Gen, don't get God mixed up in such as this. Let the doctors do their own work. Keep religion in its place."

"Which is — what?" I questioned.

"Oh, human relationships and social reform."

"But Jesus said, 'I am come that they might have life and have it more abundantly,'" I insisted. "Life is within the individual. It is necessary to have something within ones self before a person can give worthwhile help to others. Certainly Jesus spoke of human relationships and social reforms, but he also healed people's spirits, their bodies and their sick minds. Wasn't his total ministry to bring to mankind the life abundant? Many doctors and psychiatrists are finding that physical and mental ills are not unrelated to man's soul and spirit. Wasn't it Carl Jung, the great Swiss pioneer of the age of psychology, who said he had not had a patient over thirty-five years of age whose problem was not basically a religious one?"

"Perhaps he did, but let psychiatrists delve into people's minds. They are trained to do this." Stan tossed off the reply.

"Such conditions are too common to dismiss lightly," I insisted. "A child may feel condemned by his parents because of some misdeed and bury this hurt, which may affect his whole life."

"Then when he becomes an adult, we analyze him and divide him into segments and turn that area of his life over to a psychiatrist," Stan commented ruefully.

"Of course this is the day of specialization but don't you think efforts are now being made to consider the man rather than merely his physical illness or his emotional problem?" I asked. "Life is a synthesis. We can not say of any part, this is man."

"But the medical doctor may see an infection in the flesh and say, this is what ails the man. The psychiatrist may analyze him and think he has found the man's trouble while the clergyman may invite the person to church to find the answer to his needs." Stan insisted.

"Life is elusive," I offered. "It can never be completely grasped in a test tube, a theory or a dogma. Like an exquisite flower, when the blossom is torn apart, its essence is destroyed. One may say, here is a calyx, here is a petal and there a stamen, but the wholeness of the flower, which is its beauty, is lost. No longer do we sense its delicate color, symmetry of petals, fragile grace and exquisite perfume. The lovely thing we have admired is destroyed."

"Nicely put," Stan commented.

"Life is like that," I went on. "We see the material body but the personality, the invisible quality of life that shines through the flesh, the charm and sparkle, the life essence, is more than the body. It can be the harmonious blending of all a person's being as spirit gives light to all. We need well functioning glands, nerves and muscles but we also need a peaceful mind which reflects poise within ourselves, with our fellowmen and with God."

"So you are writing a psychological treatise on the Mind," Stan commented.

"Psychology does not include that which I have found to be most helpful in releasing memories of traumatic experiences," I answered. "Many doctors agree that most mental illness results from the disturbed emotions. This, in reality, may be soul sickness of the patient. Since the human being is an interacting relationship of body, mind, soul and spirit, that which deeply disturbs any of these, also affects the whole. While a psychiatrist can lead his patient to understand the cause of his illness which results from broken human relationships, only God can forgive sin and free the depressed person from his burden of guilt. Drugs may give temporary relief from hypersensitiveness, tension and worry, but only God can release the soul from deep seated fears and give peace that passes understanding. God, who made us, is able to mend our broken lives."

"But you use psychological terms," Stan insisted. "Where did you learn them?"

"I have been fortunate to enjoy a close relationship with my nephew who is a psychiatrist," I answered. "He has taught me much about counselling, has directed my reading, taken me to lectures by noted doctors and cooperated with me in the work I am doing."

"Do you mean Ernest?" Stan's eyes sparkled as he leaned forward eagerly.

"Why, of course, you knew Ernest!" I exclaimed.

"I should say I did. He was a handsome fellow in medical school when I was a gangling kid. I used to adore him and think the greatest thing in the world would be to look like him and be in medical school. So he is a psychiatrist! Splendid! Ernest must be a broadminded man to accept that which is outside his own line of training," Stan commented.

"I have found doctors to be most understanding," I answered. "Those whose greatest desire is for the welfare of their patients, are glad when they recover promptly. When prayer enables them to be optimistic and hopeful this contributes to their well being and hastens recovery. Wise doctors know that there is a Power beyond their own, that while they can dress a wound and apply medication, the Life Within the Body must bring about the healing.

"Ernest used to ask me to describe a healing which came about through faith and prayer. I did so, as accurately as I knew how, and he said that this healing process was exactly the same as that which occurred while under medical care, or as a natural healing. It seems that God has definite laws and does not break them, but as Ernest pointed out, a Divine healing usually is greatly accelerated. While a natural healing may require weeks for the body to be restored, a Divine healing may take place in a much shorter time. As Albert Einstein pointed out, time and space are relative. So they are related to this planet earth. God is not so restricted."

"But this does not lessen the value of the work of doctors," Stan said.

"No, it does not," I agreed. "Surely all who give their lives in the interest of healing are working and studying to know more of truth. Perhaps God allows us to experience Divine healings to show us that He is Truth. God, who gives us minds, certainly intends that we shall use them. Persons who do research and give to the world new knowledge for better living may touch a source of knowledge beyond human wisdom. Inspiration comes, but who can say where it comes from?"

"Of course nobody knows the reaches of the Unconscious Mind," Stan mused. "The very word implies unknown."

"Carl Jung said that we cannot possibly know the limitations of something unknown to us," I agreed.

"Some speak of a Universal Mind as if all minds may have a common source, as the fingers are joined together in the hand. Who knows where inspiration comes from. The same ideas seem to crop up simultaneously in various countries of the earth." Stan commented.

"Surely our Subconscious Minds are our silent

partners." I agreed. "Into this great working powerhouse we drop our dreams and desires that they may be empowered and brought to fulfillment. Creative workers, writers, musicians, inventors, and those who explore new realms of thought draw upon the powers of the Subconscious Mind. Did you ever work on a problem until you were weary, then lay it aside and suddenly have the answer come to your mind?"

"Yes, I've done that," Stan brightened. "I have worked on a problem until I have been exhausted, then laid it aside, and later, while I am relaxed, reading or walking, the answer suddenly will pop into my mind. Such answers often come while I am shaving."

"That is reasonable. You have given your best effort to the problem, then released it while you slept, and as you busied yourself in the morning in carefree routine, the answer came. It is a deep well of knowing — this Deep Mind of ours."

Stan's eyes narrowed meditatively. "An enforced rest seems to give the Subconscious Mind an opportunity to bring forth inspiration. I have read that Albert Einstein grasped the most momentous concept of this age, the relativity of time and space and the nature of reality, while he was in bed with an illness, or recuperating from one."

"Yes, and Christopher Morley, the writer, found that while reclining, reading detective stories, his best ideas came to him. Pasteur made his great discovery of immunization against disease through what might be called an accident caused by an assistant. But this came after Pasteur had given long, untiring effort to this research.

"Frederick Banting, a young surgeon, who gave to the world a means of controlling diabetes, from which millions had died and for which medical science could find no means of control, made his great discovery after working untiringly on the problem, then releasing it. He had worked on a lecture, he was weary, his mind a confused maze of theories, experiments and case histories. Utterly spent, he went to bed at a late hour. At two o'clock in the morning he woke up, turned on a light and wrote three sentences: 'Tie off pancreatic duct of a dog. Wait six or eight weeks for degeneration. Remove residue and extract.' Turning off the light he slept. So, there came the answer to the problem which long had baffled medical science, and countless numbers of people suffering from diabetes have been given life."

"Beethoven said he heard music while he was relaxed," Stan went on. "And Handel had gone through a period which he called dryness, when he was not able to compose a note, when, as if beyond himself great strains of music came to him so rapidly that he scarcely could write them down. This was the music of the celebrated Messiah."

"But all these men had been struggling with the problems for which they found the answers," Stan observed. "It seems that such inspiration does not come to idlers."

"You are right," I agreed. "I believe Pasteur said something of this sort; 'Chance is on the side of him who is prepared.' Still, the art of relaxation seems to invite inspiration. People who hurry all the time seldom receive such inspiration. These come most often after we have worked diligently to charm them, then wait, happily relaxed, so that they may steal in upon us unaware. Great ideas waft in, like the wind that bloweth where it listeth."[1]

"But, that was said in reference to the Spirit." Stan said.

"The Great Unconscious, the Great Wisdom, the Life Within; all have surrounded and sustained us throughout our lives. Would it be unreasonable to think that the Divine Spirit might touch our lives during the years of

---

[1]John 3:8

our highest development and give us inspiration?" I said.

Stan picked up a book, thumbed through it, then laid it aside.

"There is a place where inspiration stops and man must work out his problems," Stan made the summation.

"But when man believes God, His power can vitalize his body, his mind and his spirit," I insisted. "Wouldn't it be a powerful force in healing if the patient recognized this truth and would lend the power of his mind toward the rebuilding of his body."

"The will to live is a powerful factor in recovery from illness." Stan suggested. "I have heard doctors say that sometimes when everything seems in the patient's favor and he has every evidence of recovery, he may just die, while other patients, with all the odds against them, will get well. The will to live, or the lack of it, seems to be the determining factor."

The back doorbell interrupted our conversation.

"The man who is to work in the garden must be here," I said.

Selecting some papers I handed them to Stan, "You might look these over while I tell him what I want done. Here is some information Ernest gave me on the influence of the mind on human behavior. There are also some stories of friends who have allowed me to use them. Excuse me. I shall be back soon."

3

Barriers in the Stream of Life

BLESSED IS THE MAN WHO . . . IS LIKE A TREE PLANTED BY STREAMS OF WATER, THAT YIELDS ITS FRUIT IN ITS SEASON, AND ITS LEAF DOES NOT WITHER. IN ALL THAT HE DOES, HE PROSPERS.

Psalm 1:1, 3 (R.S.V.)

Stan read:

Life is a stream. Infancy a spring whose waters drop from rocks to form a pool and overflows in a rivulet. Youth is a brook, sparkling and dancing on its way; maturity a river that grows broad and deep as it flows toward the sea. When life's development is unhindered the stream flows smoothly, expanding in breadth and depth. But when obstacles dam its course its waters divide, and may spread over lowlands or sink into the ground. Human life can be damaged by barriers that thwart its development. When this is done emotions may become frustrated, mental powers weakened, reason twisted and the purpose of living lost. Memories of hurtful experiences may be barriers which dam the stream of life. Such memories usually are crowded into the dark area of the Deep Mind, or Subconscious, where they can produce stress sufficient to affect the health of both mind and body. It is well that we understand the various areas of our minds, so that we shall better know ourselves.

At birth the baby's body is functioning automatically through the reflex mechanisms which are built into the more basic parts of the mind. The baby has had no contact with the outside world except the traumas and emotions of the mother while it was in the uterus. These have started a beginning of its relationship with others. After birth it is not as fortunate as some animals. It is not able to care for itself and is completely dependent upon those about it for satisfying its needs for food, shelter, love and protection. Through its contact with its environment it perceives a friendly, loving atmosphere or an uncertain or hostile world.

The baby is born with certain basic drives or instincts which come from what we call the unconscious mind. These seek expression. At an early age the baby experiences the world around it. It develops and adjusts to this world. This adjusting, maneuvering, thinking, realizing and planning part of the mind that develops, we call the consciousness.

This consciousness becomes the buffer between the drives of the unconscious and the outside world while it also becomes the coping mechanism with which it deals with pleasures and pains, hardships, problems, and misunderstandings with people and situations.

The more loving, appreciative, open, and free the environment which enable the child to understand the restraints placed upon it, the more wholesome will be the child's development, both at home and at school and play. The greater the development of the conscious mind in regard to its stability and adaptability the more sure is the child's foundation of life.

Comparative areas of the Conscious and the Unconscious Mind might be made by drawing a large triangle to represent the Unconscious or Subconscious Mind then drawing a line across the tip of the triangle to make a smaller one to represent the Conscious Mind. The illustration of an iceberg floating in the sea is also used, its nine tenths below the water representing the Subconscious Mind and the one tenth above the water, the Conscious Mind.

The Mind is one, however, and the Conscious and Subconscious work together like capital and labor. The Conscious Mind might be likened to an executive. Here is the power of thinking, reasoning, planning, purposing and willing. The plans of the executive are sent down to the Subconscious Mind which might be called the construction engineer, who acts upon the ideas given it. While the Subconscious Mind uses material sent to it by the Conscious Mind it has great power over it for it may refuse to act upon suggestions given it. This is true when the action called for is associated with some experience that has caused pain to the Subconscious. The Conscious Mind may have forgotten the hurtful incident but the Subconscious does not forget. Incidents which have caused deep emotional feelings are most likely to be indelibly impressed on the memory for feelings are stronger within us than reason.

The deep Mind, or Subconscious, seems to be a filing cabinet where every thought, act and experience of life is stored. Yet, the deep mind is not static like a filing cabinet but rather, as ever moving waves of the sea, it continually washes up onto the shores of remembrance fragments of past experiences. Every day of our lives we are sending material down to our deep minds. Although an incident may be lost from the Conscious Mind it remains in the Subconscious, a powerful influence in our thinking and behavior. We are directed by our inner urges, while these are colored by our experience with the outside world. Altogether, this constitutes the basis of life. On this basis we act. The circle widens until it takes in the world about us.

The Subconscious mind influences our actions, as well as governing the functions of our bodies. It influences our nerves and emotions. This explains why our faces get red when we are embarrassed, why we get sick at the stomach when repulsed, and why we get cold and shaky when we are frightened. Powerful interaction; we entertain a thought, this produces an emotion and the emotion causes a physical response.

Although the Conscious Mind tries to forget, the Subconsious does not forget anything. So every new experience we meet becomes colored by the memory of experiences which were comparable.

When an object is pushed down into mud and buried there we can not see the object that is buried but we see the bulge of mud where it was pushed down. Such bulges indicate a person's sore spots. They are the doctor's lead to the cause of his patient's illness. As more and more unhappy memories are pushed into this area, it becomes so unpleasant that the Conscious Mind shuts out recognition of it and tries to deny that which is hidden there. As we refuse to admit the light of recognition and fail to incorporate these experiences into our lives, shrinking from them because we do not want to face them, they ferment a toxin potent enough to make us ill.

Children who are continually criticized and scolded, without love, whose efforts bring them no word of approval, usually react in one of two ways. One type may become belligerent, rebelling against parents, school and civil authorities. Such as these become the outlaws of society. Feeling the world is against them, they fight back. Since feelings are more intense than reason they strike out even at those who would help them. Such as these fill our jails and penitentiaries.

The second type are the submissive ones. These usually remain within the framework of society but are stunted. Like a tree that has been whipped by storms until its branches are twisted, such persons often are warped in their thinking. Fearful, they draw back and become secretive. Their self-confidence is weak. While they seldom hurt anyone, they lack the self assurance to succeed at anything. These are the defeated ones whose energy is spent in dodging the blows of life, runners in life's race with both feet tied together.

The hurts felt by a child often are out of proportion to that which an adult might feel. A child's world is small and when his world is shattered his whole life is broken up. The fact to remember is this: the emotional impact of a childhood trauma remains in the Subconscious Mind of the individual with the same emotional impact of its first occurence, even throughout years of adult life, or until it is understood and released. Emotional experiences pushed into the deep mind and buried there, evoke an emotional response in us whenever we face a situation of like nature in later years.

We have failed and we dare not try again.

We have fallen and we are cautious.

We have been hurt and we are fearful.

Betrayed, we dare not trust.

Beaten in competition, we shrink from rivalry.

Whipped by larger persons, our self confidence is injured.

Scolded, we cower.

Made to feel we deserve to be punished, we try to punish ourselves.

The more traumatic experiences a person has in which he is unable to cope, the more prejudices and biases he has. Intolerance of the wrong doings of others indicates a similar weakness in ones self.

A person who thinks he has no such weaknesses might answer the following questions. If he must answer in the affirmative to many of these, he should examine himself to find the cause of his responses.

Do certain people rub you the wrong way?

Do you bristle when some topics are discussed?

Do you avoid certain topics, persons, or places?

Do you feel sorry for yourself because you have been mistreated?

Do you feel the world is down on you, that nobody loves you?

Do you mull over grievances?

Do you draw away from people, fearing they may hurt or overshadow you?

Do you feel people do not understand you?

Do you feel you are not appreciated?

Do you feel you never can do things as well as others?

Do you feel that the weight of the world is resting on your shoulders?

Are you hesitant to speak your mind when you feel you are right?

Do you give in without standing up for your rights?

Do you justify all your reactions as the result of the way you have been treated?

Are you afraid to start a project for fear you cannot finish it?

Do you shut up like a clam, or explode like a volcano?

Do you feel poor and unworthy?

Do you long for the good things of life, but feel they are not for you?

Do you think mishaps are punishment meted out to you?

Do you dream of a Utopia far away, and draw away from the world about you?

Persons who have such attitudes, while not mentally ill, surely are suffering from emotional stress. They should experience greater freedom after understanding the cause of their problems and overcoming them.

The foregoing information, written by a Christian psychiatrist, should help in understanding persons who suffer from mental distress, and also enable us to see ourselves and act wisely to overcome our weaknesses. Let us begin by being tolerant of all persons who suffer, realizing we might act as they do if we had endured such experiences as theirs. Let us also realize that many persons suffer from causes they could not prevent.

This was forcibly impressed upon my mind while attending the British National Guild of Health which was held in the University of London. The general theme of the conference was concern for the mental and emotional distress among their people. Those in attendance largely were medical doctors, psychiatrists, nurses and members of the clergy. One psychiatrist voiced concern for the youth of London, saying there were among them a number who seemed unable to relate with others, who acted as if they were dazed, stunned or shocked. The persons who met in the discussion group, which I attended following the lecture, agreed with the speaker, saying these were persons who were children and babes in arms at the time of the bombings of London. They had been snatched from their beds, rudely wakened, and carried through the streets as fires lit the sky and sirens screeched, while buildings crumbled around them as they made their way to bomb shelters. In these shelters the very atmosphere was tense with fear. The little ones could not understand what was happening and were shushed into silence when they asked. Having lived through such nights of fear, which partially paralyzed their minds and emotions, many of this group were so emotionally scarred that they are unable to relate to life in a normal way.

It is not necessary to undergo traumatic experiences

as serious as those suffered by the children of London during the air raids of World War II to realize that people all about us, even we ourselves, have peculiar quirks of character which may result from some past experience we may have forgotten, or tried to forget.

I used to wonder why Sid Smith, head of a great organization, with a large number of men under him, could be as ruthless as he was at times. He seemed to need a whipping boy, someone on whom he might vent his anger and lay the blame for his failures. The explanation was clear when he told of being the youngest of five boys, and always seethed with anger when he was forced to the bottom in every skirmish.

An efficient business woman who had a phobia of riding in an elevator and walked up three flights of stairs every day to the office where she worked, could not understand her aversion to small enclosures until, through help, she was enabled to recall an experience which occurred when she was three years old. She had been playing in a closet when an older person walked by and shut the door, then left the house. The child, shut in this small, dark place, cried, screamed and banged on the door until someone came into the house and let her out. This woman took her courage in both hands the first time she entered an elevator after she understood the cause of her phobia, but soon all evidence of it had left her.

Often persons do not try to overcome an experience that seems to be a trivial thing. For instance, I was having lunch with a friend and noticed she did not eat the beets on her plate. I asked her if she did not like beets.

"It's a funny thing," she said, looking out of the window.

"Something happened when you were a child?" I asked.

"I must have been seven or eight," she said, laying down her fork. "A little friend had come to spend the night with me. There were fresh beets for supper. That night, all my mother's efforts to make beets a part of my diet were shattered. My friend looked at the beets on my plate with the red juice around them. She wrinkled her nose and said as if she were gagging, Do you eat those things? They look like blood. Somehow, I never have cared for beets since."

This was an incident. The only ill effect was that this woman lost the nourishment of a healthful food. Other experiences often are more hurtful.

Another friend told me that all her life she had become ill when she suffered the slightest burn. The sight of a burn on another person affected her the same way. She could stand cuts and bruises but a burn literally put her to bed. She knew this was irrational but was not able to account for her reaction nor to control it. Finally she consulted a psychologist.

"Have you ever been badly burned?" she was asked.

"No, I never have," she answered.

"Have you ever seen anyone who was badly burned?"

"Not that I remember."

"Go back in your memory," she was told. "Something may come to you."

She visited an older brother who remembered and helped her to recall an experience which occurred when she was five. Now she remembered when her older sister Ann was terribly burned. A pan of grease caught fire on the stove. Ann grabbed it and ran toward the door. But on the threshold she stumbled and fell. The hot grease spilled on her arms and chest.

The child had been so frightened that she crawled under the kitchen table and refused to come out, even when her mother coaxed her. The sight of the flaming grease, of the sister falling, the screams of pain and the ensuing excitement and distress of the family all blended into a terrifying nightmare which stunned the child into a panic of fear.

Later with nothing to remind the child of this

experience, for Ann's burns had healed without leaving scars, the emotional effect of the trauma became separated from its cause and attached itself to all situations involving burns. In this case the trauma affected the woman's body in its response to burns. Traumas that affect the mind are much worse than those that affect only the body.

Alice Wentworth, a college professor, seemed poised and efficient when I first met her. She was flawlessly dressed and made an effort to be friendly, yet there was a reserve about her that kept people at a distance. I later learned that all her life Alice had worked to prove to herself that she was worthy of attention and approval. The pattern of Alice's life can be seen in the following story.

Alice felt shabby as she saw her cousins in their pretty dresses. They seldom met except at Christmas when all the aunts and uncles brought their families to Grandfather's for the annual dinner. Grandmother insisted on keeping this family custom. Dinner was all the traditional Christmas dinner should have been. During the afternoon the adults visited while the children played.

This year Alice was even more aware of the difference between her family and the others. She was older now — almost eight — and she wanted very much to be accepted by them. When Aunt Myrtle suggested that they be entertained by the children, Alice tried to think of something she could do.

She watched Helen swish her ruffled skirt as she went to the piano to announce the number she would play. When Helen had finished there was loud applause and comments of praise. James did a tap dance, Edith spoke a piece, little Bobbie lisped a verse that brought laughter and praise as he ran to his mother who hugged him proudly.

"I want to say a piece," Alice whispered from behind her mother's chair where she was standing.

"You don't know any piece," her mother whispered.

Alice searched her memory for something she could say. Yes, she did know a piece. She had learned it at school.

"I have a piece," she heard herself say as she walked into the circle of relatives. She dared not look at her mother, but walked to the piano where the other children had stood. All eyes were upon her. They seemed to be closing in upon her. She swallowed hard and looked at the circle of eyes.

"Twinkle twinkle little star, how I wonder —", she began. A lump was in her throat, she could not go on for the words had vanished. She blinked, ducked her head and twisted her skirt.

"Twinkle twinkle," she began again, "How I wonder — how — wonder — wonder — ", her face was drawing in strange contortions.

Someone tittered. Then there was a burst of laughter. Everyone was making fun of her. Alice looked imploringly at her mother, but on her mother's face she saw only outraged pride. An agony of blackness was coming upon her. As the laughter rose Alice ran from the room. Like a hunted animal, she looked for a place to hide. Upstairs she found a dark closet with a low chest in it. There she sat weeping as if something deep within herself was dying.

Her parents found her there when they were ready to start home. Shamefacedly Alice went with them to their battered old car.

"What did you have to make a fool of yourself for?" her mother began as soon as they were out of sight of the house.

"Trying to show off," her father bit off the words. "Acting like a smart aleck. I'll whip that out of her. No kid of mine is going to be a smart aleck."

The wounded child quivered as she shrank from the punishment that awaited her at home.

Alice was a mature woman, poised, beautiful and efficient when I met her. She was successful in her profession, but the little girl — almost eight — crouched in fear in this stiffly proper woman who had exerted every effort to prove to herself that she could do things as well as other people. She had attained success but success was not satisfying. The child crouched in her deep memory knew no compensation, nor was it consoled.

Some years ago, during an Armistice Day celebration, a Jewish man, who had been nailing up some signs, stood before a store window in which there were displayed various relics from World War II. In the forefront of the window lay a German officer's helmet and sword. As people passed along the sidewalk, suddenly the man crashed the window with the hammer he carried, and knocked the helmet across the room. Immediately there was a buzz of voices as people gathered around. The man stood as if dazed, then he went into the store and apologized to the owner for the damage he had done and asked if he might pay for it immediately.

When this man was a little boy he had been in a Nazi prison camp. He had seen his father herded into a box car and hauled away. His mother had died of starvation in the concentration camp. The memories of those awful days were seared in his mind, until after years of covering them over and trying to forget them, they suddenly became alive as he looked at the German helmet. The little boy suppressed within the man, suddenly assumed power over him, became master of the situation and gave expression to the hate and revenge he had long wanted to let loose. The boy broke the window, the boy within the man of Jewish blood, who usually walked sedately among his neighbors.

4

Accept the Child You Were

...A BRUISED REED HE WILL NOT BREAK, AND A DIMLY BURNING WICK HE WILL NOT QUENCH; HE WILL FAITHFULLY BRING FORTH JUSTICE.

Isaiah 42:3 (R.S.V.)

Sitting quietly, the manuscript in his lap, hands limp beside it, Stan did not move as I entered my study. When he spoke, his voice seemed to come from a distance.

"Aunt Gen, did you purposely open up all this to show me myself? You know how Albert lorded it over me and how Dad treated both of us."

"He was a bit hard on you boys," I admitted.

"Al and I have a good relationship now," Stan insisted.

"Is it genuine love, or a civil courtesy?" I asked.

Stan studied the ceiling for some minutes then asked, "Have you seen symptoms of repression in me?"

"Not until I saw you so tired after your morning service."

"Do inner repressions make a person tired?"

"They often have that effect."

Stan cleared his throat. "I thought I had looked at this subject quite philosophically, but these stories got under my skin. I thought I had forgotten the hurts of my childhood, but I guess I had just covered them up. This probing hurts. I don't like it."

"No one does. It is painful like an explorative thumb pressing on our sore spots. Some can't take it. They scream and deny the truth rather than go boldly into the Subconscious and uncover what is hidden there."

"I guess I'm just human."

"I did not mean to hurt you, but it is better to face the truth than to ignore it."

"I had better face it!" Stan exclaimed, rising quickly and striding about the room. Stopping at the south windows he stood, hands thrust in pockets, a figure of grim determination. After some minutes he swung around.

"I am glad you put your thumb on my sore spot. I needed it, although it hurt. For years I have been throwing up a barrage, trying to act poised and carefree when I was not. I have tried to cover my feelings of inadequacy that I had drummed into me when I was a child." Stan's voice quavered as he turned again to the windows.

Silence filled the room.

Presently Stan turned. "How do I get at this?" he asked.

"Be kind to yourself," I said after a pause. "Think of yourself objectively. Look at the child you were from the viewpoint of the man you are now. You would not blame a child for doing things that are normal for a child of his age to do. Realize that the boy you were did as well as he could with his immature understanding."

Without speaking Stan turned away.

Measuring my words, I continued. "If the boy is father of the man, as poets tell us, then there lives in every man something of the boy he once was. Make friends with this little fellow you once were Stan. Love him. That is what he is starved for — love."

"You're telling me," Stan muttered.

Walking across the room he dropped in a chair and sank into silence. Finally he spoke. "How can you love the little guy when most of the hurts of life came through him?"

"We remember the hurts while we forget our pleasures," I answered. "As you realize, all the happy experiences of life have come to you through this same little guy. Why heap onto this little child all the hurts you remember while you forget he afforded you your happy experiences as well as your opportunities for growth? Didn't he furnish you your laboratory for learning?"

"Guinea pig," Stan grunted.

"Anyway, you learned." I smiled.

"Some of those experiences were later than my childhood." Stan's face flushed. "During my teen age Dad seemed to find some sadistic satisfaction in slapping me down."

I held Stan's eye for a minute, smiling reminiscently, then commented, "It is hard for an old cock to listen to a young one crow."

Returning my gaze while a sheepish smile crept over his face, Stan mused, "I guess I was a little cocky."

"Kids show off in order to attract attention, and attention is another term for approval and love." I said. "Our hunger for love is second only to that for food. The normal actions of a growing child are like the stretching of a fledgling's wings. He is trying to learn to fly, to use his own wings. It is his effort toward growth and self assurance. God approves of the birds' growth, and He approves of the development of children. As His children we should be confident of His love."

"It would be wonderful if you could believe God cared, then, or now," Stan spoke bitterly.

"Rather than condemning God, let's see what we can do for ourselves." I suggested. "Our attitudes at the time we were mistreated, as we feel we were, probably have been retained in our Deep Minds from the time of the incident that hurt us. They remain there because we do nothing to get rid of them. Can we expect God to go into our memories and take these attitudes from us while we cling to them? God works with us, not in spite of us, or against our will. Think kindly of the boy you once were, love him and go back in memory until you find him, crouching in fear and filled with a sense of unworthiness. You have shut this child from yourself because you have tried to forget the hurts he felt. Each time you did this, you buried some part of your vital energy and mental ability."

"What do you do when you find the child?" Stan asked.

"Own him, recognize him as part of yourself. Lift him into the light and let him live. Doesn't he cower because he felt disapproval? The longing for approval is the longing for love. Assure the child that you love him, that God loves him, and that he is forgiven for everything he did wrong, forgiven by both you and God.

"Having lifted the child, the segment of yourself which has been separated from you, now integrate it into your life. In this way you remove the poison of resentment which has depleted your energy and has influenced your actions toward other people.

"Since children interpret God by human behavior, many persons who have fallen below the standards set by parents, feel unworthy to approach God. They fear their failures will receive God's disapproval as they have brought forth condemnation from men. Whatever the failures and sins of adult life, the child lives in every one of us and when we come to God with the simple trust of a child, we can be sure that Christ will love and receive us as he did little ones of his own day.

"Jesus, with his great wisdom, must have known the effects of childhood hurts, which students of the mind are learning today, for the most scathing words ever recorded of Him were in reference to those who would hurt a child. He said: 'Whosoever shall offend one of these little ones which believe on me, it were better for him that a millstone were hanged about his neck, and that he were drowned in the depth of the sea'."[2]

Stan blinked, then slowly a smile crept over his face. "I guess we need human love," he said.

"Yes, we do. Every individual needs to feel secure in the love of someone; his father or mother, brother or sister, husband or wife. To feel secure in the love of someone gives us roots. A psychiatrist commented that the person who is confident he is loved has an invaluable security."

"You mean a lot to me," Stan smiled unsteadily.

"I have loved you like one of my own children. You seemed to belong in our family when you first came to play with them."

"You encouraged me without coercing me," Stan lifted his face and smiled.

"Don't blame yourself," I smiled. "Many people love you."

"Since you and God love me, I'll try to love the little guy."

"Your father loved you," I insisted, "although he wasn't able to let you know that he did. Why do you suppose your father acted toward you as he did?"

"I often have wondered," Stan said, then added apologetically, "Father is dead, you know. I am sorry to be talking about him this way."

"Yes, I know, but death does not erase deeds done during a person's lifetime. It is as necessary to forgive persons

---

[2]Matthew 18:6

who have passed from this life as to forgive those who are living.

"As I knew your father, he was a man of few words, seemingly unable to express his feelings. He was well past his youth when he married. Of course he wanted love as every human does, but seemed unable to tell his wife this. She was young, happy, and spilled her affection on everybody — perhaps more on others than on her husband. When you came along she poured her love on you."

"I'm sorry to say it, Aunt Gen, but you know Mother was inconsistent. She indulged me one day then pushed me out the next."

"Could she have been more consistent in her love to her husband? Could your father have been jealous of the love she gave you? Did he long for attention and appreciation as he saw attention lavished on you? Was this the reason he lost his temper like a dam that broke?"

"And the broiling flood waters escaped as he vented his feelings on us boys." Stan shook his head sadly.

"Perhaps he saw in you characteristics which he would have liked in himself. He may have known he would have been as sparkling and as outgoing as you if someone had not crushed the vivacity out of him when he was young. Think of what he must have suffered when a child. Then the rule was, 'Spare the rod and spoil the child.' "

"And he practiced it," Stan spoke sadly. "He vented his anger on us boys. Al couldn't strike Dad, so he vented his anger on me."

"And now, the figure of your older brother appears in persons who annoy you by seeming to lord it over you." I commented.

"So, you've seen how Lee Masters rubs me the wrong way," Stan smiled ruefully. "I am ashamed of allowing that man to get under my skin as he does, but there is something about his very presence that burns me up. The trouble must be in me."

"Come into the kitchen," I said, rising quickly and leading the way from the room.

"Refreshments?" Stan asked, following.

"Strong ones," I laughed.

"Sit there," motioning toward the kitchen table, I turned to the vegetable bin and took out an onion which I put on a plate and set on the table.

"Oh, no!" Stan exclaimed. "You tell me life is a flower, then you put an onion before me."

"Life isn't always as sweet as a flower."

"I hope it isn't as smelly as an onion."

Stan looked up and we broke into laughter like children freed from an emotional strain.

Cutting the outer layer of the onion, I soliloquized, "Life is composed of layers like an onion. Each ring of the onion might represent a period in a person's life. Let's say this is the life of a man — a hypothetical person.

"Now, what might have happened in the life of this man recently to blight his peaceful existence?" I asked, pulling the loosened outer ring away from the onion.

"Umm, suppose he ran for a political office and was defeated." Stan entered into the game.

"And the defeat caused a bruise on the onion — I mean an emotional reaction in the man. Now, what might have happened in the life of this man before that?" I cut another layer of the onion and drew it back.

"Let's say he was in line for a promotion in his business firm and another man was promoted over him."

"Another bruise," I agreed, peeling the onion more deeply. "And what might have happened before that?"

"Maybe a shyster sold him a gold brick and he has seethed with resentment against this man, and against himself for being taken in." Stan's enthusiasm carried him on.

"Say, you are making things hard for this fellow," I laughed. "But all such experiences of the adult life can and should be dealt with by the conscious mind, the will, and reason. It is hurts of childhood which are retained in the subconscious mind."

"The first day he went to school the bigger boys ganged up on him and watched while a kid two years older and twenty pounds heavier beat him up." There was feeling in Stan's voice as he went on, "His self-respect was hurt worse than his bleeding nose, and he never forgave those boys, nor forgot that he is a whipped child." Stan's voice showed that he was no longer speaking of a hypothetical man.

"You see, all these hurts contain some resentment. But even so, it is through our deepest anguish that we attain our glorious victory," I smiled up at Stan.

"Oh, I must run!" Stan exlaimed as he looked at his watch. "I am due for an appointment this minute! I'll be back. We must continue this discussion. Bye now."

5

The Lord Is in His Holy Temple

BUT GOD, WHO IS RICH IN MERCY, FOR HIS GREAT LOVE WHEREWITH HE LOVED US . . . HATH RAISED US UP TOGETHER, AND MADE US SIT TOGETHER IN HEAVENLY PLACES IN CHRIST JESUS:

Ephesians 2:4-6 (KJ)

There was no response to my tap on the door of the church secretary's office. Then, as I turned away, a muffled voice said, "Come in." All thought of the item I had come to check for the bulletin, vanished from my mind as I looked at Ann, her shoulders slumped and her face red from weeping. It is not unusual for a young woman to be in tears, but for Ann Warner, poised, efficient and self-possessed to be weeping was out of character.

"Oh, thank goodness it's you," Ann dabbed at her eyes, "I was going to call you."

Thinking some tragedy had befallen Ann's family, I placed my hand on her shoulder and asked, "What has happened, dear?"

"It's the atmosphere in these offices," Ann blew her nose furiously. "The tension between Lee and Reverend Houston is getting so bad I just can't take it much longer. I am right in the middle — caught between them. They both give me orders. What am I to do? The friction is burning me up."

"Oh, I see," I said weakly, seeing more than I cared to admit.

With the look of a hurt child on her face, Ann looked up and said chokingly, "I don't know what has gotten into Lee. He is not the person I used to know. I thought I loved him, and I did, but I can't love this man he has turned into."

"How has he changed?" I asked.

"Oh, he tries to run everything. He makes plans for various class meetings and never consults Reverend Houston to see if these plans are agreeable with him. Last week Reverend Houston told a group that they would be meeting in the Wesley Room this coming Friday, then Lee put a notice in the bulletin that a class would meet there that night. That's it!" Ann flared "I get the bulletin out and Lee gives me items for it that cross up the plans of the preacher. It seems that Lee takes delight in needling him."

"Have you talked to Lee about this?"

"I have, and Lee just laughs like he is doing something smart. I can't understand him."

Ann rose and walked about the room, drawing deep breaths, then went on, "When Reverend Parkins was pastor here he liked for Lee to attend to details and let him act as kind of church manager while he gave his attention to his sermons. But Reverend Houston knows that this church is his responsibility and he intends to look after it. He always is courteous but sometimes he is cool and curt, so austere he almost frightens me.

"Now don't tell me to pray about it," Ann cried, "I would rather bump their heads together."

I repressed the laughter which seemed inappropriate at this time, "Of course, Ann, prayers need willing minds and the use of hands and feet to put them into practice. Usually we should do more than pray."

"What can we do?" Ann looked up.

After thinking a moment, I suggested, "Let's you and me join in surrounding these men with light. Let's put each of them in a capsule of God's light and keep them there. We can visualize Divine Light all around them as the yolk of an egg is surrounded by the white. Divine Light is the warmth of God's love, His wisdom and His guidance. As we hold Lee and Reverend Houston in this light we shall give thanks that God is working in their lives to bring about His will in them."

"Will this work?"

"It has worked for others, it should for us."

"I'll try it," Ann smiled faintly, "I'll try anything that will help."

As I neared the chapel where the Tuesday morning prayer group met, strains of music floated out. Mrs. Fleming was at the organ, playing as the women gathered. After a devotional meditation and prayers, I was asked to lead in the sharing service. Facing the group I smiled.

"Who has a happy experience to share with us?" Looking at the smiles that lit up these friends' faces, I went on, "We rise higher through praise and thanksgiving than in any other way I know of. Let us magnify the good and think much of God's love and mercy. The Psalmist said, 'Oh, magnify the Lord with me and let us exalt his name together!' To magnify is to make large, you know, so let us increase the good about us by expecting it. We help to bring into being that which we earnestly desire and give power to that which receives our mental energy.

What answers have you had to the prayers you prayed last week?"

For some minutes there was hearty response, then Mrs. Arnold spoke in a regretful vein, "I think we should pray about a situation that exists in our church. I work in the youth department and I am sorry to say it, but Lee is leading these young people to believe the morning worship service is not important, that their classes and parties are all they need."

"There is friction between Lee and the pastor," another affirmed.

So, the friction among the church staff was spreading through the congregation. I must have wisdom and guidance. Like the Psalmist of old, I silently, cried unto the Lord, and the thought that came to me must have been inspired. Looking up I smiled in assurance of my guidance.

"A person traveling over the fruitful plains of western Oklahoma could hardly believe that this land of lush pastures and waving grain could once have been so dry that topsoil was whipped into the air to produce what was called the Dust Bowl. At that time my husband was appointed District Superintendent over this area, with fifty-six churches under his supervision. Many people had left the land and moved away, but those who remained were persons of strong character, tenacity and fortitude. They evidenced courage and optimism which was heroic.

"Often I went with my husband as he visited these people. He was a young man, but it took a young man to meet the challenge of those days. Also, he has a contagion of courage which seemed catching as he moved among people. While he talked with men in their places of business and in their fields, I met with the women of the churches. Discouraged and impoverished, they looked for some ray of hope, and often would say, 'Oh, Mrs.

Parkhurst, talk to us.' What could I say? I could not tell them of the apportionments they were supposed to meet for work in the mission fields, for they were worse off then many the Church was supporting. I could only turn to God for a message for discouraged people, such as these. And God gave me an answer."

"What was it?" Mrs. Allen asked eagerly.

Joy filled my heart as I remembered His blessings in the yesterdays. Knowing that His mercies are ever new, I said, "Instead of telling you, suppose we join in doing what these women did in their grief and discouragement. Remember how God revealed his presence to Isaiah in his hour of need," I said. "His friend King Uzziah had died, and besides his grief at the loss of his dear friend, Isaiah felt concern for the welfare of the nation. So he turned to God in the time of his trouble and went into the temple to worship. As he sought God with his whole heart, he saw God's glory filling the temple as a bright light that touched the altar and radiated throughout the place. When Isaiah realized the omnipotence of God, present even in time of distress, God spoke to him and gave him the message which made his life meaningful.

"Let us see the glory of God filling our sanctuary of worship. Using your God-given imagination, close your eyes and create a picture on the screen of your mind's eye. See our sanctuary as you see it each Sunday morning, the pastor in the pulpit, the choir, and the people in the pews. When this picture is clear in your mind, ask God to grant you the spiritual sight to see His glory in His sanctuary as Isaiah saw it. Now, visualize a white light surrounding the head of our minister, see this white, translucent light expand, growing greater until it completely surrounds the pastor, then envelops the choir, it rolls forward, covering the chancel, the first pew, the second, and on back until the whole congregation is enveloped in the white light of God's glory. It touches the windows, reaches the ceiling and fills the narthex."

"Umm," someone breathed, then all was silence.

"We should go to church to worship God rather than to hear a sermon. As we are conscious of God's presence in the sanctuary we are enabled to do this. One person who prays during a worship service blesses that service. A group praying and visualizing God's presence in their midst can so change the atmosphere of a place that God's Holy Presence is felt by all who are able to respond to His inspiration.

"When a minister feels the presence of God's Spirit upon him as he stands to preach, his mind is quickened, his heart warmed and he is able to proclaim the message from God as a true prophet of God. When hearts are warmed and thoughts uplifted a congregation is drawn together as they respond to the highest aspirations of their own hearts and the inspiration of the service. It is then that God is in His Holy Temple and is able to make His love and will known to His people."

Blended together in thought, the women sat in silence as minutes passed. No one moved for we seemed to be welded together in a holy hush.

"Thank you Father," I whispered.

Deeply drawn breaths broke the silence, yet no one spoke.

"How many were able to visualize the picture?" I asked. Every hand was lifted, Soon many were asking about the experience.

"All right," I quieted the group, "let us do this next Sunday. Before you enter the sanctuary pause an instant the renew the vision. Say in your heart, 'Dear Lord, while I will not be able to see your glory with my physical eyes, I shall see it with the eyes of my spirit and I shall know you are in the sanctuary today.' After you are seated close your eyes for an instant and recapture the vision. Repeat this during the service. Now, be careful not to tell other people what we are doing. Power is lost when sacred things are exposed."

"Will this work?" someone asked.

"It has been effective in many groups," I answered. "Churches divided by rifts have been brought together, preachers have spoken with unusual power, and love has overcome hatred when God's Spirit has been revered in His Sanctuary and in the hearts of those who worship Him."

"Oh, I would like to do this," Mrs. Evans cried, and a number joined in agreement.

"We are going to find that this will help us individually as well as helping our congregation and our pastor. We shall truly be in the Spirit as we sit together during our worship services. This will be a good time for us to send out rays of Divine Light and Love to various persons whom we see around us. Persons who look sad or troubled will be blessed as we radiate God's love to them. And if there is anyone whom we do not like, or with whom we have had trouble, we can ask forgiveness and beam love to her. God may be able to give us his grace so that we can do more than this."

"When shall we begin?"

"Right now," I answered. "Each week as we come together for prayer we shall close by visualizing God's Presence in our sanctuary. Then each Sunday morning, before entering the church, let us pause to make sure we are in accord with the Spirit and submit ourselves to His guidance. Let us do this for six weeks or two months at least."

All agreed and we departed with the determination of a high purpose.

Martha Manning joined me as I left the church and

asked if she might talk with me some time soon. Wondering what was troubling Martha, I told her to come to my home the following Friday afternoon at two.

6

A Hurtful Memory Is Released

I HAVE BLOTTED OUT, AS A THICK CLOUD, THY TRANSGRESSIONS, AND, AS A CLOUD, THY SINS: RETURN UNTO ME: FOR I HAVE REDEEMED THEE.

Isaiah 44:22 (KJ)

Martha was on time for her appointment. She sat down, straightened her skirt, placed her handbag on the floor beside her, then took it up and sat holding it tightly.

"I hope I'm not bothering you," she spoke apologetically.

"Are you feeling well?" I asked.

"Yes, I am quite well physically but there is something else — I hate to mention it, you have done so much for me, but I can't overcome it."

"You can tell me about it," I said kindly, moving closer to her. "If I can help you I shall be glad to do so."

"Yes, I know," Martha faltered. Then she raised her head with determination. "I get my feelings hurt so easily. It seems I can't take criticism at all. Rebuff of any kind just kills my soul. When anyone is unkind to me my face gets red, I'm all aflame inside and it is all I can do to keep from crying. I am ashamed to act this way. I'm forty-three years old and I know better than to act like a baby, but I can't help it."

It might be that some deep hurt during her childhood was causing Martha to react to criticism as she did. I spoke kindly. "When our reaction to any situation is more intense than the situation warrants, it is helpful to go back in memory and to see if there is some experience in the past which is triggering off our emotional feelings," I said.

"How can we do that?" Martha asked.

"The cause of your sensitiveness may lie deeply buried in your subconscious mind," I answered. "Have you tried to associate it with some hurt you suffered as a child?"

"I don't remember anything."

"It may be buried so deeply that you can't remember it, or it may have happened when you were too young for conscious memory to recall it. The Conscious Mind is kind. It often blocks from memory things that are too painful to recall."

We talked together for some time as I explained to Martha the workings of the mind as my psychiatrist friend had told them to me. I knew Martha so well that she trusted me and responded to my directions.

"Lie down on the couch and relax," I said. "Slip off your shoes and loosen any tight clothing."

"Am I going to sleep?" she asked.

"No, just relax completely and if you can, allow yourself to drift into the state between sleep and waking. We shall try an experiment in prayer, with the help of the Holy Spirit who is the "Gentle Mother" of the Trinity. We shall ask that the Creative Power which brought you into life shall open the closed area of your mind and permit you to see what lies hidden there which is causing you this trouble."

"That sounds far out," Martha protested.

"No, it is very simple," I assured her. "Let go of all your fears and inhibitions and be a little child again. Rest as relaxed as a baby in its mother's arms. God is Divine Mother as well as Father. This holy love that brought you to life knows every thought that ever has been in your mind, knows, and loves you as dearly as if you never had thought an ugly thing."

As Martha lay on the couch, I placed my fingers gently on her temples as I prayed that the Holy Spirit might bring to her remembrance any forgotten hurt that might be thwarting the life of this, God's child.

Martha's breathing became even and light.

"You are doing well," I said. "Now let your whole life roll before you on the screen of your mind, only let it roll backward. When you see something there, describe it — talk it out. You are not talking to me, but to God. I shall not listen especially, and whatever I do hear will be kept secret."

After many minutes Martha began to speak. Her voice came as from a far distance — snatches of sentences, half-heartedly spoken. This went on for some minutes. Then she began to cry. The crying turned to sobs. She sat up, weeping, as great sobs shook her body. She got up from the couch and walked back and forth across the room, crying as though the depth of her being was broken up.

I sat still, waiting.

Finally Martha blew her nose, wiped her eyes and came back to the couch. "I know what it was," she moaned, "I saw it. I lived it all over again."

"That is good," I said.

"Good?" she cried, "It was awful!"

"It is good that you relived it. Now you can bring it out and get rid of it. Until now this memory has been sealed in your Deep Mind but hidden from your conscious memory," I explained.

"Shall I tell you about it?"

"That might help you."

"It was when I was about three years old," Martha began, then she gave way to another spasm of weeping. "I don't know if I can tell it," she said chokingly.

"Take your time. There is no hurry."

"I was just a little thing," Martha began again. "I loved my mother more than anything. I wanted to let her know how much I loved her. One day I found some pretty flowers. I was glad, for I could take them to her to show her how much I loved her. So I picked the flowers. I had both hands full of the blossoms. As I went toward the house I saw my mother on the porch. I was all glad inside as I thought how pleased she would be with the flowers I was bringing her. I ran to her and smiling happily I held up my hands filled with the blossoms." Silent sobs shook Martha's body. "This was my moment of joy," she went on after a bit. "But it was a brief moment. When mother saw the flowers her face turned to fury. She screamed at me. She slapped the flowers from my hands. She slapped my hands as she ranted in a high voice. She was giving a party the next day and had cultivated those flowers carefully and was going to use them on her tables. Now I had ruined every one for I had picked the heads off so there were no stems.

"I stood aghast, petrified at her rage. I had anticipated approval. I had come in love and was scolded. Now she slapped my face, first one side then the other until I bobbed from side to side between her stinging hands. Mouth open, I was unable to move. Then she turned and went into the house and banged the door behind her and left me outside."

Again the little child, which had come to life in the forty-three year old woman, began to sob. "Why am I crying like this?" she said.

"Because the little child, so long crushed inside of you, is coming up for air. She has been buried in your Deep Mind for years. You are feeling now as the child felt then. Let her live again. Allow her to express those feelings and bring them to the surface. Don't repress her any longer. Give her air."

I remembered a psychiatrist saying that rejection from love is the most devastating trauma a child can experience. This child's love had met hate, her offering had brought punishment. Hurt, disappointed, rejected, she was utterly alone and shut off from love when the door slammed and shut her outside.

"Did you cry when your mother shut the door and left you outside?" I asked.

"Cry? Of course!" Martha looked at me in surprise. "How could I help it?"

"Then cry now. Relive the emotions of this child and experience them again. This will help you to forget them as you wash them out of your Subconscious where they have been locked and have created the reaction that has made you so afraid."

"My God," Martha breathed, and her words were not profane. Can it be possible that this hurt has been deep inside me all these years?"

"Yes," I answered. "The emotion you felt then has risen through the years whenever you have been hurt. The child in you has cowered, afraid to meet people, anticipating rejection."

"Oh, I know it," Martha wailed.

"This traumatic experience has caused you to be shy and unduly sensitive to offense. You have felt hurt many times since you were three years old. No doubt there has been a chain reaction of hurt feelings throughout the years. As a row of dominoes, standing on end, will fall when the end one is pushed, this childhood experience has been the end domino that has triggered off a series of hurt feelings." I explained.

"But I had forgotten that experience. I didn't remember it at all until I lay down on this couch," Martha protested.

"You have responded to it throughout the years, haven't you?"

"Yes," Martha admitted slowly.

"Then some part of you remembered. While your Conscious Mind forgot, your Subconscious remembered and caused you to feel much as the child of three felt and to act much as that child would have acted."

"Oh, this is so distressing. It has wrung the life out of me." Martha sobbed.

As I saw Martha's distress, an idea came to me. Could Martha visualize the Christ Presence, I wondered. I have been cautious about offering this method of prayer-cleansing to people; doing so only after prayerful guidance. I never would suggest it to anyone whom I felt would not receive it reverently and in faith. Yet, to those who have been able to understand and enter into the experience the results have been, at times, miraculous.

"Martha," I spoke hesitantly. "Were you able to see this incident of your childhood as it rolled before your mind's eye, or did you feel it and think or imagine how it was?"

Martha hesitated. "It was overpowering in its reality. I may have seen it — yes, it was visual to my mind's eye, but the great impact was the way I felt it. Why?"

"Will you try to use your mind to bring another picture

into reality? Persons who do creative work use their imagination. Anyone who is able to use this mental faculty constructively should be grateful for it. Will you try to create a mental picture, with the use of your imagination?"

"I'll try, if it will help," Martha agreed.

"Close your eyes, relax, become quiet, quiet and receptive." Martha lay back on the couch.

"Think of the mothers who brought their children to Jesus and of how he took the little ones in his arms and blessed them."

Martha nodded mutely.

"See if you can reproduce this scene on the screen of your mind. Think of Jesus sitting on a rock beside a dusty country road. Imagine the blue sky above his head, perhaps some floating clouds. See the rough landscape, rolling hills with dwarfed scrubby bushes. Think of the road near him running over the hills in the distance.

"Now, imagine a group of women coming over the hill and approaching Jesus. The women are chatting as they walk. Some are leading children while others carry babies in their arms. Other little ones run ahead of their mothers as the party moves forward."

"Yes," Martha breathed.

"Now the group approaches Jesus. Think of the look of kindness on his face as he rises and greets them. Love flows from him like sunshine. Feeling this love, the children run to Jesus. See him take a baby in his arms, hold it lovingly as he gives it his blessing, then return it to its mother's arms. Now he stoops and lifts a small child who has been standing near. He gently lays this little one on his shoulder as he speaks softly, patting its back. It lays its head confidently on Jesus' shoulder and nestles against his breast, content, happy."

Martha was quiet, breathing lightly.

"Can you feel this love of Jesus?" I asked.

"Oh, yes," the words were half sob.

"Transfer this scene to another time and place, but do not lose the central figure, Jesus. Hold the vision of Jesus in your mind but now see him standing beside a little girl crying on the ground outside a closed door, among scattered blossoms."

Silence. Then a choking sob, "Oh, he is there. He is."

"Allow him to lift this little one to his breast. See her lay her head confidently on his shoulder. The child is no longer crying, for infinite love is flowing into her and healing her hurt."

Presently Martha sat up. "He did! He did just that," Martha's eyes were shining. "I felt his love go through me. I imagined the visual part at first, then it became plain, but I felt his love. It is real!"

Slowly Martha rose and walked about the room. "He loves me, He loves me," she affirmed, from the deep assurance of her heart.

"And this love draws the hurt from the child you were," I said assuringly. "Now can you forgive your mother and forget the hurt? Reliving a past experience with Jesus is more helpful than telling it to another person."

"Oh, yes, I can," Martha said. "God draws all the hurt out of the child I was, and from the person I am now. I feel all clean inside." Smiling, she went on, "Like God's promise to remove our transgressions from us as far as the east is from the west, it seems that Jesus removed this transgression from me, even my feeling toward my mother."

Again Martha was silent. After a thoughtful pause, she turned to me and asked, "Why doesn't God take these hurts from our deep memory when He forgives our sins?"

"When we ask God for pardon it is for the sins we have committed. These hurts are the result of sins committed against us. In the Lord's Prayer we pray, 'Forgive us our trespasses as we forgive those who trespass against us.' As we are forgiven, we need to forgive. Sometimes we must forgive before we are forgiven," I answered.

"Can everybody see Jesus with their mind's eye like I did?" Martha asked.

"Not everyone has such a vivid mental vision as you have, but everyone can receive Jesus' love by faith, as we receive our salvation," I answered. "We are told, 'The just shall live by faith.'[2] You remember, Jesus was especially interested in Thomas, the doubting disciple. He did not criticize him, but said, 'Be not faithless, but believing'.[3] He also said, 'Thomas, because thou hast seen me, thou hast believed; blessed are they that have not seen, and yet have believed.'[4] Even though we are not able to see with our mind's eye, we can reason. We have Jesus' promise, 'Lo, I am with you alway, even unto the end of the world.[5] Perhaps it is even better to believe with faith than to see with the mental vision." I smiled. "When we accept God's promise with our will and our reason, we are allowing the mind of Christ to be in us, as Paul advised us to, 'Let this mind be in you, which was also in Christ Jesus' "[6]

"Am I going to be completely freed from this childhood trauma?" Martha asked.

"Haven't you been building a habit pattern for forty years?" I asked.

"Yes."

"Then can you expect to completely erase that habit pattern in an hour?"

Martha smiled.

"Works of divine grace are much alike," I went on. "One

[2]Romans 1:17
[3]John 20:27
[4]John 20:29
[5]Matt. 28:20
[6]Philippians 2:5

who has been a sinner for forty years may have a marvelous conversion experience, yet it takes much faith, prayer, and effort for him to overcome the habit pattern of his past. During the time of overcoming, he is sustained by the reality of his conversion experience. This same memory of Christ's work of grace will sustain you as your former habit pattern grows less and less binding until at last you are free of it."

Martha turned to me, smiling, "You have helped me to release this trauma. I wonder — is it possible for a person to do this by himself?"

"It is possible," I answered, "but it is better if you have someone to share the experience with you. This person should be one who has faith in God and in prayer and one whom you love and trust. Love is the frequency on which healing operates. As we have said, love is expressed by approval and acceptance. The person you choose to help you should be one who will not criticize or condemn, but who will understand and love you."

"We do a lot of things we regret after we are past the days of childhood," Martha mused. "If all our mistakes were made in our infancy it would be simple to release them and absolve ourselves from gnawing regret, but this is not the case."

"As long as we live we shall make mistakes," I agreed, "but each time we make right a wrong we can congratulate ourselves that we are more mature and more Christian than when we blundered."

"Go forward in the sustaining assurance that we are God's children and that His grace is sufficient for us. As great and as perfect as the Eternal is, Paul said that His strength is made perfect in our weakness," I added.

"Does that mean that God needs us so that His grace may be manifest through us?" Martha asked. Then smiled, "If it does, then we really are important, aren't we?"

7

Your Idea of God Is Important

BEHOLD, WHAT MANNER OF LOVE THE FATHER HATH BESTOWED UPON US, THAT WE SHOULD BE CALLED THE SONS OF GOD . . .

I John 3:1 (KJ)

Cool shadows from swaying leaves interspersed the green of the lawn, flower beds lifted many colored blossoms, a robin cocked a quizzical eye as he hopped nearby. The only sound here on the terrace was of a few cars passing on the street at the far side of the house.

Stan sat with face lifted toward the treetops and the impenetrable blue beyond. When he spoke it was as from a great distance. "Aunt Gen, God is real to you, isn't He?"

I watched him lean forward and pick up a maple leaf which he seemed to be examining carefully. "Yes, Stanley," I answered softly.

"Tell me what God is."

"Why, you graduated from a theological seminary," I countered.

"I seem to have lost Him — as a reality — as you know Him."

Tossing the leaf aside Stan turned toward me, his lips grim. "I must be honest. I have gone along with you — or allowed you to go on — acting as if I agreed with all you said. But I cannot. I do not think of God as I did when I was a child."

"That is natural," I agreed. "Our comprehension should increase as we grow older."

"I do not think of God as having any concern for what I, or any other mortal does. I can not believe there is an Intelligence which hears when I pray."

I sat silent, waiting.

"Of course God is the Creative Force, the First Cause, the *Elan Vital,* a Power, unknowable." Stan paused, then finished with a wry smile, "I know all the words but I seem to have lost the music. You are so confident, so sure, it haunts me." He turned away. "I suppose it is my fault, I am not blaming anyone, theological training is predominately intellectual — theological and intellectual in emphasis, rather than spiritual. Little attention is given to the training of the spiritual life. It is taken for granted that each student is spiritually equipped when he enters seminary, and it is up to him to maintain his individual prayer life. With the pressure of study, this often is neglected. One gets out of the habit of praying. Prayer comes to mean auto-suggestion, or talking to ones self. Many drop it altogether."

I waited quietly.

"A deep loneliness pervades the lives of many clergymen. They do not speak of it, but it is there like quicksand beneath the foundation of their faith."

Silence hung between us.

Now Stan turned and looked at me intently. "Tell me, Aunt Gen, what God is to you. You have tested Him in the crucible of living."

"What do you believe, Stanley? What do you believe concerning Jesus?"

"He was a good man, a teacher."

"But not the Son of God?"

"No more than other men."

"And His miracles?"

"They can be explained as natural happenings or as exaggerated tales told by excited onlookers."

"Do you believe in Immortality?"

"It is doubtful."

"What do you believe — that you can preach?" I pressed.

"I believe in brotherhood as Jesus taught it. The world can use much of that. I can preach what Jesus said about human relations. If I preached about a God who answers prayer that would be putting on an act, a farce. I will not do that."

Stan shifted his position and spoke in a lighter tone, "I try to say something in my sermons that those who do believe can interpret to satisfy themselves. People hear what they want to hear, largely."

I prayed that my experience in counselling would enable me to give positively through my feeling of empathy. Here was another young minister who had gone from a small church where the power and presence of God had touched his life and had led him to choose the Christian Ministry as his life work, who had finished college and gone to a theological seminary with high hopes that there he would be prepared to preach the Good News of the Gospel of Jesus Christ, only to find that he must say, as did Mary on Easter morning, 'They have taken away my Lord, and I know not where they have laid him.'[1]

"It is difficult to realize that the Creator of all things has an interest in you and me," I said. "The Universe testifies to a creator, but our hearts cry out for something

---

[1]John 20:13

more, for some love that will fill the void in our lives. People of all tribes and cultures have lifted their deepest yearnings to some sort of a god, but only Jesus gave the revelation that God is Our Father. Since God is Spirit, as Jesus said it may be that the eternal spirit of man relates to the Creator more closely than the material things of his creation do."

Stan sat drumming his fingers on his chair arm, a faraway look on his face.

"Psychologists tell us that children live through the various stages of development through which the race has passed. Would this growth be comparable to man's evolving comprehension of God? The Bible seems to reveal an unfolding understanding of God, such as a child might feel toward his parent as he grows up.

"The baby's first need is for food, protection and love. The mother gives these. To the infant these are all of his mother. She may be a singer able to hold her audience enraptured by her voice, or a writer of such ability that her readers eagerly await the publication of her books, but to her baby she is only milk and comfort. This is all of the mother her baby can comprehend and it is all he needs to know. At this stage of the child's life little is expected of him. He delights his parents when he laughs, coos and throws his hands as they talk to him. The parents desire that their child recognize them and that he shall grow, nothing more. When we are infants in the faith, this is all Our Father expects of us.

"As the child grows he may think of his parents as ones who give him gifts and toys. When his father returns from a trip, the child meets him crying, 'What did you bring me?.' He goes through his father's pockets in search of some gift.

"Early in our Christian life we think of God as the giver of every good and precious gift, most of which are to us material things. But let us not despise the Christian of this age. Jesus promised things to his followers. Did he not say, 'Seek ye first the kingdom of God, and his righteousness; and all these things shall be added unto you'?[1] Our trouble is that we want things before we have attained 'his righteousness.'

"The young child goes through a stage of possessiveness when he may cling to his mother and cry, '*My mama!*' He wants his mother as his own, regardless of other children in the family. Wasn't there a time when the Israelites thought of Jehovah as their tribal god and prayed he would avenge their enemies — and these were all the people around about them? Now we know that God is God of the Universe.

"When the child reaches the age when his explorative ventures must be curbed he may think of his father as a disciplinarian. Was there not a time when the Israelites talked of God's wrath and His vengeance upon those who displeased Him? Wasn't it He who thundered in the heavens causing them to quake before his rage? Was this a true picture of God, or wasn't it rather the conception of Him held by a people stuggling in growth?

"The child of ten is so absorbed in his play that he scarcely can take time to eat. He comes when called, wets his hands and wipes them on a towel, gulps his food in haste to return to his game. He gives no thought to where the food came from, or who pays the rent or taxes on the house that shelters him. Life is the fun of living. Many people have reached the spiritual age of ten years and seem to have no desire for further development. Few families, in this land of plenty, bow their heads at table and give thanks for their food.

"During adolescence youth often is carried away by the

---

[1]Matthew 6:33

discovery of new truths. A boy in his early teens, making experiments in a chemistry laboratory, may become so absorbed in his findings, that for the time being he thinks of nothing else."

Stan grinned as he remarked, "Maybe our whole nation has reached the adolescent age which is the time of competition in sports in which teams as well as individuals strive to prove their strength. Our Space Program is a competitive race with another nation and our rockets to the moon certainly have been a spectacular demonstration of our success. This is good, as I see it, but these nations are showing a higher development by sitting down together to discuss their differences. Maybe the world is growing up, after all its struggles."

"Thank you for your optimistic note," I smiled. "Yet I fear there is much growing to be done before wars are outlawed. Human greed and selfishness motivate the thirst for conquest. Is it possible that man ever can overcome these by his own efforts alone? Is this not our need of God? It seems that God created man incomplete without Him. Augustine put his finer on man's frantic searching when he said, 'Lord, Thou hast made us for thyself, and our hearts are restless until we find our rest in Thee."

"Then you feel that God is not a force afar off," Stan concluded.

"God is the wellspring of our very being, the essence of our best selves, God in us." I replied.

Stan looked at me for a long minute, then asked, "How do we allow God to become that to us?"

Picking up a book I had been reading I turned its pages thoughtfully.

"Dr. Alexis Carrel, in his book *Prayer,* wrote so beautifully about man's approach to God and how best we can find Him. He says: 'It may be that we reach God better through love than through learning. True prayer represents a mystic state when the consciousness is absorbed in God. This state is not of the intellectual nature. Also it remains as inaccessible, as incomprehensible to the philosopher and to the learned. Just as with the sense of beauty and of love, it demands no book knowledge. The simple are conscious of God as naturally as of the warmth of the sun, or the perfume of a flower. But this God, so approachable to him who knows how to love, is hidden from him who knows only how to understand. Thought and word are at fault when it is a matter of describing this state. That is why prayer finds its highest expression in a soaring love through the obscure night of the intelligence.' "[1]

"Let me see that book," Stan said.

I handed it to him, and he read silently for some time. When he laid it aside he remarked, "This was written some time ago."

"Is it possible that the nature of God and of man has changed radically in the last few years?"

"Dr. Carrel's ideas differ from those of this country," Stan went on. "Although he made outstanding accomplishments and won the Nobel Prize while he lived in the United States, he spoke from a universal point of view. He was a man of many nations, spoke a number of languages and wrote fluently in at least three, you know."

"Yes, and he makes this point," I replied. "He also said, 'To us men of the west, reason seems very superior to intuition. We much prefer intelligence to feeling. Science shines out, while religion flickers.' "

"Wait a minute," Stan protested. "That man is touching a vulnerable spot."

"He goes on to say, We seek first of all to develop intelli-

[1]Prayer, Alexis Carrel, Morehouse-Barlow, N.Y. Copyright 1948.

gence in ourselves. As to the non-intelligent activities of spirit, such as the moral sense, the sense of beauty, and above all, the sense of the holy, they are almost completely neglected. The atrophy of these fundamental activities makes of the modern man a being spiritually blind. Such an infirmity does not permit him to be an element good for the constitution of society. It is to the low standard of the individual we must attribute the collapse of our civilization.' "[4]

Stan rose slowly, "That hits where it hurts," he said, walking about the terrace, then returning to his chair he sat, looking at me expectantly.

"God has been interpreted in many ways," I went on after awhile."To the ancients, God was a force to be feared. To the Hebrews, God was law. To some, God is Divine Mind or Principle, but to the Christian, who takes as his source the words of Jesus, God is Our Father."

"Of course, the parent-child relationship is the closest we know, for like begets like," Stan agreed.

I nodded and went on, "While the human body is part of God's creation, it is man's mind and spirit that are most like God, for 'God is a Spirit.'[5] In order to understand God, we strive, as Paul said, to 'let this mind be in you, which was also in Christ Jesus.' "[6]

Stan had risen and was pacing about the terrace. Pausing, he looked at me and asked, "Is it necessary to believe that Jesus was the divine Christ, the Son of God, in order to most fully comprehend God?"

I was silent for some time.

Stan rejoined me in his chair, and waited.

---

[4]PRAYER Dr. Alexis Carrel, Morehouse-Barlow, New York. Copyright 1948.

[5]John 4:24

[6]John 14:6

"From time immemorial men have worshipped gods of some sort," I said. "The word, god, has various meanings, to different peoples. Only Jesus revealed God as Our Father and he said, 'No man cometh unto the Father but by me.' "[7]

---

[7]John 14:6

8

What About Jesus?

AND THE WORD WAS MADE FLESH, AND DWELT AMONG US, (AND WE BEHELD HIS GLORY, THE GLORY AS OF THE ONLY BEGOTTEN OF THE FATHER,) FULL OF GRACE AND TRUTH.

John 1:14 (KJ)

We sat in silence for some time, then Stan asked, "Aunt Gen, did you really see Jesus as you wrote in your book, *Healing and Wholeness?*[1]"

I looked at Stan wonderingly. Did he doubt my truthfulness? With bated breath, in memory, I relived the marvelous moment when Jesus stood before me, and with eyes full of compassion and love, yet with all the majesty of Him who created the Universe, looked into mine, and I was instantly healed.

"Yes, Stanley, I really saw Jesus," I answered softly.

"I don't doubt that you thought you saw him," he said, "but it could have been hallucination or an illusion."

"Would a malignancy vanish before an illusion?" I asked.

---

[1]Macalester Park Pub. Co., St. Paul Minnesota and Arthur James Limited, Evesham, England.

Stan moved uneasily. "No, I suppose not."

"No, Stan, it was not hallucination." I said firmly.

As I looked at this young minister, trained to preach the Gospel of Jesus Christ, I wondered why men work so hard, bringing to bear every available argument to disprove the divine life of Jesus and explain away all his miracles. Their explanations often are more incredible than the simple fact that the power of God was upon him.

"Why do you think you had such an experience?" Stan asked.

"I have wondered," I answered. "It certainly was not that I was worthy." I lapsed into silence, thinking.

Stan looked up questioningly.

"You remember the story of Daniel in the lion's den," I said, "and how the king who had allowed him to be placed there was troubled and could not sleep, how in the morning he went to the den and cried out, 'O, Daniel, servant of the living God, is thy God, whom thou servest continually, able to deliver thee?'[1] There are many persons who do not profess the Christian faith, yet who hope there is truth in that which Christians believe. The world is watching the Church today, hoping that the God we serve is able to deliver us — and them. Doesn't the Church need a restoration of faith in the power of the God whom we serve?"

Stan nodded but did not speak.

"I am of the Church. I love the Church. As you know, my father was a minister and so is my husband. I have lived my life in the Church. Can it be that God gave me this experience so that I might witness to the Church that His power is as great today as it ever was? This thing I know," I said emphatically, "Christ Jesus is a living presence in the world today!"

---

[1]Daniel 6:20

Stan's face was flushed, his lips drawn tightly together.

"As the unknown power which we call electricity is condensed and made available for man's use, so Jesus is the transformer which brings the power of God into availability to mankind. A condenser turns vapors into solid form. It is a lens which concentrates light." I paused, feeling for words. "Yes, this is what Jesus is, a transformer that makes the immensity of God comprehensible in terms mankind can understand."

Stillness enveloped us. Stan sat quietly looking at me. I went on speaking — to whom? To myself? It did not matter to whom — merely speaking the words that flooded my mind. I seemed impelled to speak. "Jesus was the Word made flesh who dwelt among men so that they saw, 'the glory of God in the face of Jesus Christ.'[1] The *Word,*[2] as used by John in the beginning of his Gospel, is the best translation the English language has for the Greek word *Logos* but it denotes only a fragment of the meaning of this word which was used by John as he described Jesus. For *Logos* means not only word but speech, treatise, discourse, science, principle of the world's coherence and reason. This then, was the all-comprehensive mind of Christ whose spirit was embodied in the human man, Jesus."

"Jesus is accepted as a good man," Stan offered.

"Yes," I agreed, "Jesus was a good man, but there have been many other good men. He was a wise teacher, but there have been other wise teachers. He was an interpreter of life, but others have interpreted life. He was a great philosopher, but other great philosophers have lived. His greatness was himself for the essence of the Godhead was reflected in him. His teachings were not mere words he

---

[1]II Corinthians 4:6

[2]John 1:1

spoke, but the expression of His being. Jesus' words came alive in his actions." I went on, "Christ Jesus is forever ahead of man's highest attainments. We may rise to a new plateau of social advancement and feel quite proud of ourselves, then we realize that nineteen hundred years ago Jesus expressed the ideals embodied in our reforms. Wherever we are we find that Jesus is out beyond us. Jesus' greatness can not be measured by what he *did*. His work is not finished. His greatness is manifest by what he *started*. That which he began is going on. His influence is not a memory but becomes more powerful with the passing of time."

I glanced at Stan who sat looking into the distance.

"Christianity is not merely an ethical teaching," I continued. "While it gives the world its highest code of ethics, it imparts to those who receive it the Spirit of Him who taught these ethics. Christianity is not only a social order, although the Church affords social fellowship which is a basic human need. Christianity, truly lived, brings into being a social order that lifts humanity and changes social relationships. It is not an escape from present unhappiness to a future heaven, although through Christ we have the assurance of immortality. Christianity is the power of the Living Christ in the lives of His followers in the world today."

I paused, but Stan made no response, so I went on.

"While Jesus was here in the flesh he could associate with his disciples and talk to those who crowded around him, but after he ascended he was among his disciples and those who believed on him as an invisible, yet very Real Presence. So he is with us today. Radio and television carry voices around the world. To hear them it is only necessary to have an instrument which is in tune with the broadcasting station from which these voices are speaking. Could this not be true of the phenomenon called prayer?"

"What would you say is Christianity's greatest contribution to society?" Stan asked.

"Isn't Christ Jesus himself Christianity's greatest contribution to the world?" I asked.

"Why hasn't Christianity permeated the world more than it has?" Stan questioned.

"Can it be that many who profess Christ accept only such parts of his teachings as agree with our own beliefs and suit our desires or pleasures while ignoring the others?" I asked. "E. Stanley Jones, missionary of world renown, says that the world does not want our religion but they love our Christ."[1]

"Strange thing about Jesus," Stan commented. "You think you have him catalogued, then after a talk like this, he is not under the index where you placed him. This is disturbing."

I smiled. "Can it be that we are disquieted when we try to analyze Jesus because we discover that he is not being tested but that we ourselves are in the test tube?"

Stan did not answer.

"We may think of God as Creative Force or as a cosmic blur but as we look steadily at Jesus he probes into the depths of our being. He puts pressure on our vulnerable spots and causes our weaknesses to stand out in glaring light. Our racial mind, our 'Old Adam' cringes before his gaze. Then it is that this thing in us rises to fight. Something has to die! Either he or it. So we cry, 'Crucify him!' Kill his divinity. Make him a man as I am — no better than myself. Then I can save my savage selfishness and call it normal human instinct. Then I can look at him and not be uncomfortable."

Stan moved uneasily in his chair.

"If we fully accept Jesus as Christ, the Son of God, our racial consciousness must become subservient to Him

---

[1]Used by permission of Dr. Jones

as he is permitted to be first in our lives. Is this the dying to self which is necessary before we can be *one with him as he was one with the Father,*[1] as he prayed at the close of his ministry? This was Jesus' supreme desire for his disciples. Surely he knew that without the power of God's spirit filling them they would fail."

Stan was frowning, his face flushed.

"Everyone who seriously encounters Jesus must make his own decision as to who Jesus is." I went on, "When the crowds that had followed Jesus turned away from him he looked at his disciples and asked: 'Will you also go away?' Then it was that Peter answered for himself and also for every generation that was to follow when he said, 'Lord, to whom shall we go? Thou hast the words of eternal life.'[2]

"Jesus speaks softly. He does not compel. He says, 'If any man *would come* after me,' implying that each person must follow of his own free will, 'let *him* deny *himself,* and take up his cross, and follow me.'[3] It is up to each of us to make his own decision — to accept or to deny. His words are quietly spoken, yet they cause conflict within us, for we are forced to decide the question, 'What shall I do then with Jesus which is called Christ?'[4]

"Jesus is central to the Christian faith," I continued. "God promised He would come into the world. Prophets foretold his coming and after his death and resurrection the Holy Spirit which came on the day of Pentecost, referred back to him. The mission of the Holy Spirit is, as Jesus said it would be, to bear witness of Jesus, bringing to remembrance the words he spoke, and empowering

---

[1]John 17:21
[2]John 6:68
[3]Matt. 16:24
[4]Matt. 27:22

those who follow him, to carry on his work. Jesus did not begin his ministry until after the Holy Spirit had descended upon him, and said he did nothing of himself, but that which the Father directed him to do.

"The cross is the strong ridgepole that upholds all the Scriptures, those which were before him, and all that has come after. The Christ, God's gift to the world, gives mankind access to the heart of the Father."

Stan turned to me, paused meditatively, and said, "Aunt Gen, if I honestly believed that Jesus was the Divine Son of God and that his Spirit is an active, Living Presence in the world today, it would change my life and revolutionize my ministry."

9

Relief From Thorns That Fester

BLESS THE LORD, O MY SOUL, AND FORGET NOT ALL HIS BENEFITS: WHO FORGIVETH ALL THINE INIQUITIES; WHO HEALETH ALL THY DISEASES.... WHO SATISFIETH THY MOUTH WITH GOOD THINGS; SO THAT THY YOUTH IS RENEWED LIKE THE EAGLE'S.

Psalm 103:2, 3, 5 (KJ)

A few days later Martha returned. "I am so happy to have relief from that thorn that was festering in my memory," she began. "You have no idea how good it feels to be rid of it. I've been thinking about the things besides childhood experiences that stick in our minds, like fears and hates and sins and foolish things we've done and just plain boneheads we can't forget. A lot of people have memories like these and would like to be relieved of them."

"What a descriptive illustration — thorns that fester," I smiled. "I remember the time my little girl ran a sliver deep into the thick of her hand. I tried to pick it out, but failed. The hand got red. That sliver had to come out. It was poisoning my child. I would have to take her to our doctor, perhaps have the hand lanced. I made one more effort to extract the hurtful splinter. Now, amid tears and prayerful effort the sliver was out. I breathed a thankful relief as I held the offending bit of wood in my hand and looked at it. It was not large, in fact it seemed a small thing to have caused so much pain. But I felt relieved when I had the splinter in my hand, glad it was no longer imbeded in the flesh of my child."

"What if you don't feel you are forgiven after you have confessed your sins?" Martha asked.

"Ask yourself why. Be honest. Have you really forgiven everyone who ever hurt you, or are you laying the blame for your hurts on others? Only a strong character can shoulder the blame for his troubles, and will stand up and say, I am to blame. Perhaps there are no more difficult words to utter than, 'The fault is mine,' and, 'Forgive me.' God has not left His people without help but has instituted the Church and given his clergymen the power to forgive sins in His name."

Martha looked into the distance for some time, then said:"If there was anything really bad in my past I wouldn't want my pastor to know it. Every time we met socially I would remember the thing I had told him and feel that he was thinking of it too."

"You might go to a city where you are not known, and there, in a church which makes use of the confessional, kneel in the confession booth where you would not see the priest who listened to your confession as you made it to God. God's ministers are ordained to be Shepherds of the Flock and Channels between men and God.

"Agnes Sanford, in her book *The Healing Light,* deals with this well. She says:

"I had sent forth the light to so many sick and

troubled people that my own light had grown dim. . . . . 'Oh! Lord! I've got to have more power,' I prayed, 'Show me how to get it.' And He showed me.

"The confessional sets free in you the power of God through the forgiveness of Jesus Christ. . . . The suggested method was to go to an Episcopal priest whom I did not know.

"So I had my first confession. . . I followed the strict cut-and-dried form of the church. I read the opening prayer in which I stated that I was guilty of certain sins, by my own fault, by my own most grievous fault. . . . . . I was forced to look squarely at all my failings and call them sins and to accept full responsibility for the same. . . . Having read through my list, without comment, I then ended with the printed prayer on the desk before me. . . Whereupon the priest made one statement and one only. He said, 'Although few people know it, the church through Jesus Christ really does have the power and authority to forgive sins.' Then he pronounced the absolution, as I had heard it many times in the communion service, and I rose and went out.

"This was done by an act of the will and of the will only. There was no emotion connected with it except a feeling of distinct discomfort. . . . But I had hardly gone out of the place before I was flooded from head to foot with the most overwhelming vibrations. I felt a high ecstacy of spirit such as I had felt before when very spiritual people had prayed for me. . . . . I knew by the inner warmth and tingling that my nerves and glands were being healed. . . . Something touched my heart. A stream of tenderness was released in me and I knew that this was the forgiveness of Jesus Christ — His life given for me."[1]

"Oh, that is beautiful" Martha breathed.

Some weeks passed before I saw Martha again. Then one day she came looking happier than I ever had seen her.

"I came to tell you about the change that has taken place in my life since last spring when you helped me clear out all the debris that was in my basement of memories," she said smiling. "I can scarcely believe, even now, all that has happened in my change of attitudes. Things seem to assume a different light. Bringing Jesus into my past was the most wonderful experience of my life. It was so real that I never can doubt that He is a living presence among us today."

"I am glad you came, Martha," I smiled. "If you can describe your experience I shall be glad to hear it. Tell me just what took place and how you felt."

"Well," Martha hesitated, "deeply moving experiences are hard to explain. But Jesus was real, as real as if He was right there with me, which, of course, He was, for He drew all the hurt out of me when I was able to give all my feelings of rejection to Him. It must be that He assumed my hurts for they were taken away. I never have had them since. It is as if I was washed clean inside."

"That is exactly what took place. Jesus did assume your hurts," I agreed. "Often when a person consults a therapist he makes a transference of his feelings of love or hate to the therapist. When an individual fixes his trust in a human being he later must go through a weaning process to detach himself from the person who has helped him. The advantage of allowing Jesus to assume our guilts and hurts is that when a person places his faith in Christ

---

[1]*The Healing Light* Agnes Sanford Macalester Park Publishing Co.

he never needs to withdraw from the love of God. Instead this confident abiding makes his life richer."

"I do feel a greater security and consciousness of God's love," Martha agreed. "Yet, all the time, I have grown in self assurance. It has taken time, like the gradual growth of a tree or plant." Martha smiled warmly. "One of the most remarkable changes that has come is the change in my attitude toward my mother. I had retained a child's point of view. Now the relationship seems reversed. I can see Mother as she was when I was three. Why, she was only a girl then, no older than my Jane is now. She had no training in child care. What frustration she must have felt, being a wife and mother at that age. Her party was a great event to her. Probably she was to entertain friends from town and had worked until she was exhausted, cleaning and setting tables. And her flowers. . . ." Martha paused, "they must have been in the vegetable garden where the chickens could not scratch them up. Flowers were not easily come by in those days. No doubt she had hoed and watched them, hoping they would be in bloom for her big day. When I came, carrying the mutilated blossoms, it must have been the last straw. She simply went berserk — beside herself for the moment. She did not realize what she was doing to me. She never would have hurt me intentionally. I realize that now."

"How did you feel when you realized all this?" I asked.

"I felt so sorry for this tired, disappointed young mother that I wanted to take her in my arms and comfort her. A great compassion flooded over me. With this compassion came love." Martha paused thoughtfully. "Yes, that is the way it came; first understanding, then pity, then compassion and finally love. All my life Mother has tried her best to give me every advantage, while inwardly I hated her and resented her efforts as interference. My emotions toward her have been those of a slapped baby. I have reacted like a child."

"Do you feel differently now?" I asked.

"I hope my attitudes are based on understanding rather than rising entirely from emotions," Martha smiled, a twinkle in her eyes. "I think at last I am growing up."

Not all persons are able to see Jesus with the mind's eye as Martha did. Yet it seems that most Christians to whom God is a reality easily identify Jesus and him who 'taketh away the sins of the world.'

If a person is not able to visualize Jesus I usually say, "That is quite all right. Just relax. You know you did not make yourself. Just trust that the benevolent Power which created all things is watching over His creation. Certainly He is able to go with you into your past and help you to clear from the corriders of memory, the hurts you have carried from traumatic experiences. Do this with the full consent of your mind, believing God is with you. Although you can not visualize Jesus beside you, know he is sharing your griefs."

10

We Come From God Who Is Our Home

> AND THEY BROUGHT YOUNG CHILDREN TO HIM, THAT HE SHOULD TOUCH THEM: AND HIS DISCIPLES REBUKED THESE THAT BROUGHT THEM. BUT WHEN JESUS SAW IT, HE WAS MUCH DISPLEASED, AND SAID UNTO THEM, SUFFER THE LITTLE CHILDREN TO COME UNTO ME, AND FORBID THEM NOT: FOR OF SUCH IS THE KINGDOM OF GOD.
>
> Mark 10:13, 14 (KJ)

"Ah, it is good to be here." Stan smiled as he sank into a chair. "Today let's resume the conversation I interrupted by leaving hastily the day you dissected the onion. I've smelled onion ever since, when I have thought of my hang-ups. You seemed to have taken the lid off of a deep area of my life. I would like to resolve those hurts if it is possible."

"Good."

"How do we get at the cause of buried hurts?" Stan asked. "I suppose that if children were given everything they wanted and surrounded with love they might be happy adults."

"Surrounding them with love would be a good thing," I answered, "but giving them everything they want would be overindulgence, and that is harmful to the child," say child psychologists."

"Now, do tell! How do they figure that out?"

"They say that when a child is given everything he wants he is robbed of the development of his initiative and incentive toward accomplishment. Parents often try to give their children what they themselves missed in life, but the children may not develop the strong character which hard knocks and necessity produced in the parents."

"I suppose that when things come too easily none of us really appreciate them," Stan said thoughtfully. "It may be necessary to want a thing, in fact desire it so much that we are willing to work to get it, before it has meaning to us.

"I will never forget how I wanted a pair of roller skates when I was a kid. I worked at everything I could find to do and saved my nickels and dimes. I would go to the hardware store and look at those skates and count my money. When I finally had enough to buy them I was the proudest kid in town. I doubt that any automobile I ever have had has given me the thrill of ownership that those skates did."

"If the skates had been handed to you the first time you spoke of wanting them would they have meant as much to you?"

"Oh, my no!" Stan laughed. "Those were more than skates, they were evidence of my ability to buy them."

"Exactly," I agreed. "So children grow when undertaking tasks they are able to complete and their self confidence is stimulated when they are praised for their success. Approval is an expression of love."

"I suppose it is when children are criticized without praise that they feel inadequate," Stan mused, "Overindulgence may be bad but I'll take it in preference to crushing the self confidence out of a child."

"It seems that children who are overindulged by their parents run into trouble with their playmates. Because of their high opinion of themselves they tend to be overbearing. Such an attitude may carry over into adult life. The person having been given everything he wanted, expects favors and finds it hard to adjust to the world in which he must live. Such persons usually blame their parents for not disciplining them when they were children."

Stan sat, chin in hand. Presently he looked up smiling, "You can't win, can you?" he grinned.

"I suppose the parents' role is to protect and train their children to become self reliant," he continued, "to make decisions and assume the responsibility for the results of their actions, and to guide them until they are able to stand on their own feet. So, discipline is necessary."

"Ernest told me an interesting thing about discipline," I offered. "He said that when a child is allowed to do as he pleases and to think he is 'Lord of the Manor' a weight of responsibility may rest on him. When he goes to bed and darkness closes in, he may be filled with fear for he wonders what would happen if a burgular were to enter the house. He knows that he is not strong enough to protect it. This may cause the child to suffer fear that is deep and damaging because it is concealed, thus, causing him to suffer later in life. It is said that discipline need not be administered as harsh punishment but should be as wise guidance and protective restraint administered in understanding and love."

Turning to me, Stan asked, "Aunt Gen, what have you found to be the most traumatic experiences which children suffer?"

"I hate to let my mind dwell on the atrocities committed

on children," I shuddered. "Unwanted children born from sex gratification, cuffed, scolded, hated because they interfere with the parent's selfish desires for freedom to go and do as they please is worse than beastly. Animals care for their young. Such children, screamed at in anger, cowed, repressed, filled with fear, develop distrust, insecurity and hatred instead of confidence and love. The foundation of such a child's life becomes insecure for he has nothing he can believe in to hold to.

"Then there are little children in foundling homes, clinging to the bars of their cribs, looking out at persons who pass by, yearning for someone to show them the attention and love which they long for. Love is necessary to the life of an infant. Everyone who is alive has had some love or he would not be here. Babies must have love in order to live. The young of wild and domesticated animals snuggle up to their mother's body and draw nourishment from her. The rhythm of her heartbeat comforts them.

"At birth the baby is cut off from the vibration of its mother's body to which it has been accustomed during its pre-natal development, and it feels lost. The touch of its mother's hand may comfort it. To be held close to the mother's body is better. If a mother is not able to nurse her child she should hold it as it is fed from the bottle. The loving touch tells the child it is secure. Babies feel this as they are bathed, powdered, dressed and held.

"Some years ago all babies left in foundling homes were listed terminal, for it was expected they would die before two years old. It was learned that such a home in Germany did not lose its babies. A group of doctors went to this home to learn what treatment was different from theirs. They found that the babies were fed and dressed the same, but there was one thing which was unusual. Every day middle aged women came in and lifted the babies out of their cribs. They held them, rubbed their hands over their heads, rocked and sang to them. This expression of love gave life to the children. They lived because they felt loved.

"Children who have lost their mothers through death may feel deserted and desertion is a devastating trauma. Children desperately trying to find love, and failing, usually go through three stages of regression. At first they will scream and try in every way they can to attract attention. Failing this, they grow quiet, whimpering softly, and draw within themselves. While the crying may go on for several days, the whimpering fades off into quietness as hopelessness engulfs the child. Once a child has reached this stage it is difficult ever to arouse it or to bring it back to normal life."

"Oh, Aunt Gen, isn't there something happy about childhood we can think of?" Stan cried.

"There certainly is," I agreed. "Infancy should be the happiest time of life. A healthy baby who is loved is naturally outgoing, responsive and happy. He is living in his Eden.

"Many psychologists agree that each individual, in the process of growing up, passes through all the stages through which the race has come in its climb toward civilization. If this is true, the days of infancy are those of man's Eden when he was in perfect harmony with God."

"Run that by me again," Stan frowned thoughtfully.

"Can it be that there is, in the deep mind of the race, a memory, not consciously recalled, but dimly felt, of a time when the individual was in complete harmony with his Creator? Does the young child, free of human hurts, live in the other-world of Spirit before he adjusts to the material world about him? Is the little one so lately come from God that heaven lies about him? As William Wordsworth said in his 'Ode; Intimations of Immortality':

Our birth is but a sleep and a forgetting,
The soul that rises with us, our life's star,
Has had elsewhere its setting
And cometh from afar;
Not in entire forgetfulness,
And not in utter nakedness,
But trailing clouds of glory do we come
From God who is our home;
Heaven lies about us in our infancy!

Shades of prison-house begin to close
Upon the growing boy,
At length the man perceives it fade away
And fade into the light of common day.

We sat in silence for some minutes, Stan with his fingers laced together, his face lifted. Clearing his throat he spoke.

"Wordsworth says that shades of the prison-house begin to close about the growing boy. The radiance of babyhood soon fades away and is lost in the light of common day. How true.

"I don't know about the theory of each individual passing through all the stages through which the race has lived, but it sounds sensible. Boys like to dig caves, crawl into them and peer out as if they were cave men. They build tree houses and seem to relive the savagery they think of as Indians. Maybe some persons never progress higher than robbers."

"Life does seem to be a struggle," I admitted, "and our greatest conflict is within ourselves. Our higher nature wrestles with our Racial Instincts, our Old Adam or our Shadow Self. Desire for Self Preservation and the Will to Power sets man at variance with his fellows."

Stan shrugged, "It would seem that man needs to be saved from himself." A smile played around his lips and his eyes twinkled, then he commented dryly, "It must have been a very young child that Jesus set in the midst of his questioners when he said, 'Of such is the kingdom of heaven.' Man's natural cussedness soon gets him into trouble."

"True," I smiled. "Yet in spite of man's perversity he is God's creation and there must be a spark of Divine light remaining in him. Although this light is covered by darkness it creates a yearning, a striving and a restlessness. Man is continually struggling for some change which will bring something better. It is as if some inherent good in ourselves is lost, and we try to recapture the music of a lost refrain.

"God is everywhere, constantly around us in the common day of life. Yet since God is Spirit we cannot see Him. Jesus was God visible in flesh, and often is very real to children during their days of innocence. It is interesting that some persons are able to see Jesus with their eyes of spirit after they have cleared away all hurtful memories of their lives back to their infancy. If there is something here that needs washing away, Jesus may appear and make right the wrong."

The ringing of the doorbell called me from the room. Stan's look of incredibility followed me as I left.

11

God Answers an Earnest Call

AND YE SHALL SEEK ME, AND FIND ME, WHEN YE SHALL SEARCH FOR ME WITH ALL YOUR HEART.

Jeremiah 19:13 (KJ)

When I returned to the room Stan asked, "Have there been healings of the memories all the time you have been counselling with people?"

"There have been many healings of memories but I did not think of them as different from other kinds of need for some time. This story in my book *Healing and Wholeness* is interesting. Handing the book to Stan I left him to read:

> One Sunday afternoon a leading citizen of the community who was a member of our congregation, called at our home. He had the air of one with important business on his mind and intent on seeing it through.
>
> "I have a real problem," he said, "and since you believe in prayer I thought you might help me."

"I shall be glad to try," I answered.

He clapsed his fingers together, looked at the carpet as deep lines of concentration etched his forehead.

"It isn't what you'd call sin, I suppose. Not what the world would call sin, but it is a thing that is eating the life out of me."

Again he was silent and I wondered what could fit that catagory. Now he straightened up resolutely and spoke with certainty.

"It's the awful memory of the war. People who never were in the thick of battle can't possibly know what we lived through. One day we were in peaceful home, schools, and churches that taught us not to kill; then before an inner adjustment could be made, we were pushed out and told to kill. We had to make a right-about-turn and do things that all our lives we had been drilled not to do. Everything in a man rebelled against it."

Again he was silent, thinking, then went on.

"I was an officer. I had to lead my men, and I had to carry out the orders given me. It was my duty. I had to. But it was so distasteful that my stomach rebelled against the horrors I saw. Sometimes when I thought of the boys, the mere kids who had to live through it, to see it, to be part of it, I hurt deep inside. And I had to lead them on in battle.

"I don't speak of it, I keep it to myself. Most men do, I think, but it is still there. The awful horror of it grips me in the night and I live it all over again. I wake up from a dream of seeing a bayonet plunged into the breast of a youth, of hearing the screams and the agony of the dying, and I'll be in a cold sweat. Sleep is gone after that. I get up and walk. Just walk to keep from thinking. I've tried everything I know to do, but the deep memory is still there. I push it away during the daytime, but at night it gets me."

"That must be a terrible experience." I said.

"I've prayed. Lord, how I've prayed. But maybe I don't know how to pray right. Is there something else I can do?"

Now I was silent, praying for an answer. When it came I was confident that it was right.

"There is something else," I said, "something deeper than prayer, for it is beyond human effort."

"For heaven's sake tell me."

"This thing that has caused your suffering is greater than you are, greater than any single man. It is a sin of all the nations involved in the war. It is my sin as well as yours for you were fighting for my country. I share this guilt with you, but I am not able to lift it. It is too great for both of us. It is the sin of the world and we must find an approach to God which is great enough to lift the sins of the whole world."

"What would that be?" he asked.

"It is the atoning blood of Christ which was shed for the sins of the world. That is great enough. In the Atonement there is forgivness for every sin, for personal anguish and for the sins of the whole world."

"Do you honestly think so?"

"Yes, I honestly do," I answered. "Many Christians do not realize the power of the Sacrament of the Lord's Supper, Holy Communion, or the Eucharist. We observe it in remembrance of the atonement made by God's Son for the sins of the world. That includes all sins, in war or peace, for nations and individuals. The sacrament is a symbol, but it is more than that. It is a symbol of a great divine reality, the reality that God loved the world so much that He allowed His son to redeem the world through giving His life and shedding His blood for us. This is the reality, the sacrament is the symbol of it."

"You mean there is power in the Sacrament of

the Lord's Supper, the bread and the wine, or grape juice, that we take in church on Sunday morning, to lift this awful torment from my subconscious mind?" he asked, wonderingly.

"There is more power in this sacrament than we realize. There is power for our salvation, which means wholeness of our souls, minds, and bodies. Many are healed of physical illnesses through receiving the emblems of Christ's body and blood. These emblems are to each individual that which his faith believes them to be."

"You believe it would help me?" he asked.

"I do believe it," I answered. "Let us be in prayer about this matter during this week and as you come to the Communion service next Sunday morning, come with expectation. I shall be praying that you may receive all you have need of and I believe your load of guilt will be lifted, your Subconscious Mind cleared, and great release will come to you."

"That would be wonderful," he said, rising. "I'll be glad to try it."

I was much in prayer during that week and rose early Sunday morning to pray for the service. The sanctuary seemed filled with a Holy Presence as the service began. As this man walked to the chancel and knelt before the altar, I knew that it was a momentous occasion. And when he walked back down the aisle the light on his face showed that he had not been disappointed.

That afternoon he came again to our home.

"It's gone!" he breathed reverently, his face aglow.

A few weeks later he came again to say that not since he had received the emblem of the blood of Christ had he been troubled.

"It is almost unbelievable, I seem washed clean inside." he said. "I have to think to remember the thing that haunted me."

> Five years later I met him and with a broad smile he said, "That wonderful experience awes me when I think of it. The power! Just think of the power in the blood of Christ, and we go to church and go through the form of taking the Holy Sacrament. Think of all there is there and we miss it because it is only a form to us. If people only knew!" [1]

"Aunt Gen," Stan's voice sounded strained. He was looking at me intently, his face a mask of incredibility. Tapping the book he held, he spoke in measured syllables. "Do you mean to tell me there is that much power in the Sacrament of the Lord's Supper?"

I was taken back. Why should he speak so, he, who was a clergyman, ordained to administer the Sacraments of the Church?

I must answer him, but how could I make clear in everyday English the availability of God's power to His Church through the Sacrament Jesus ordained, as I knew it? Somehow words came, I seemed to hear them rather than to formulate them.

"The Sacrament of Our Lord's Last Supper is a bridge spanning man's incredibility, joining the material world with the world of spiritual reality. It is hard to comprehend Spirit in this world of matter, even though we know that our real person is spirit, living in a material body. Science has taught us to accept as truth only such as can be proven by our physical senses. When our loved ones have departed this life we remember them largely by physical mannerisms; we recall how she held her knitting needles, how he looked up over his newspaper. Jesus must have known how mortals rely on their physical senses for that which

---

[1]Healing and Wholeness, Chapter XX pages 150-152
Arthur James Limited
The Drift, Evesham, Worcs. England.

they think is real, so he told them to remember him through something as common as the material elements of food and drink.

"During that Last Supper Jesus took bread and broke it and gave it to his disciples, saying, 'This is my body, broken for you.' As he lifted the loaf they saw it. They heard the crunch of the home-baked crust as he broke it, and smelled its aroma. As the disciples took the bread given to them, they felt it in their fingers and on their tongue before they tasted it. All their physical senses bore witness to this bread.

"The wine Jesus poured must have gurgled as it passed from decanter into the goblet. It glowed red as he lifted it before his disciples' watchful eyes. Its fragrance wafted to their nostrils. They felt it on their lips and tongue and tasted the juices of the grapes.

"As all their physical senses responded to the reality of the wine, Jesus said, 'This is my blood which is shed for you. As often as you drink it, drink it in remembrance of me.'

"He gave to them bread and wine which were very real to their physical senses. The bread represented the body, the wine the blood, the life essence, and the Spirit. In so doing he was saying, I too am real, very real. I have promised that I am with you always even unto the end of the world. So I am, with you, invisible, but very real.

"At one time when I was studying ancient writings about this sacrament, trying to understand its depth, I laid my books aside and asked, "Dear Lord Jesus, what do you have to teach me about this?'

"The following Sunday I went with my husband to a small country church. Here white bread was used in the communion service. As I knelt and placed a piece of bread in my mouth, the Inner Voice spoke clearly to my consciousness, saying, 'Hold it.'

"I held the bread in my mouth, then took the juice and discovered that the bread acted as a sponge to hold the wine. The taste of bread was lost in the taste of wine.

"The Inner Voice spoke again, saying 'I would have My Spirit fill you as this bread is saturated with the wine.' From that time on I have received the elements in this way. This is the meaning of the Holy Communion to me."

Stan rose abruptly from his chair and walked to a window where he stood looking out.

Silence filled the room as minutes passed.

Quietly Stan returned to his chair and sat in meditation.

After a time I spoke. "It is amazing that God's Spirit can enter into man's Subconscious and reveal what is hidden there."

"A noted medical doctor says in a story of his own experience of healing a long-felt hurt, that he believes God will bring up from the unconscious whatever needs to be known if we ask Him."

"Who is that?" Stan asked flatly.

"Doctor Loren T. Swain, medical doctor and specialist in treatment of arthritis, says in his book, *Arthritis, Medicine, and Spiritual Laws,* that this is true. Here is the book if you care to read it."

Silently Stan read:

A CHILDHOOD HURT

An experience of my own illustrates how the lasting effects of a "forgotten" childhood hurt can be healed.

For years I had been vaguely conscious that it was hard for me to care deeply for people. What troubled me most about this was that, although I dearly loved my wife and my mother, there seemed to be a point beyond which I could not let them into my heart.

One day, returning from Europe by boat, my wife

and I were sitting in the sun and enjoying the feeling of having nothing to do. Suddenly it occurred to me to ask God why I could not care for people as I longed to do. So I did.

Almost at once my face flushed, my hands trembled, and I grew hot and angry. I was ten years old again and vividly reliving an experience I had completely forgotten. I asked a little girl to be my best girl — since each of the other boys had one. She said, "No. I like Lawrence better."

I felt again all the anger and the deep hurt to my pride. I recalled abruptly turning away. The next day her closest friend offered to be my best girl.

"No," I told her, "I don't want one — ever."

During the few seconds that I so intensely re-lived this incident I could almost hear my unconscious mind register this decision — "Never again will I be hurt like that, never will I care enough for any girl to let her hurt me."

I turned to my wife and told her the whole story. Here my past experience with others came to my aid. I knew that just seeing it and sharing it was not enough. In order to have that hurt completely healed, so as to be free from it forever, I had to bring in a Power beyond my own. So we prayed about it together, there on the deck. I gave it up completely. I asked that my ten-year-old heart, which had never grown up after that hurt, should grow up fast even if I had to suffer in the future. That day a forty-year-old buried wound was permanently healed. My caring for people has grown ever since. This release brought me closer to my wife and gladdened the last years for my mother.

Occasionally I still get hurt, but I no longer bury the hurt. I quickly admit it, give it up, and thus am free of it.

Because this happened to me, I know exactly how it came to mind and how I was afterward freed from

> its restriction. *This incident proved to me that God will bring up from the unconscious whatever needs to be known if we ask Him, but we must honestly want it, expect it, and accept it.* Furthermore, when we surrender such an incident, He will straighten out its consequences and free us from the emotional power it generates. Then it is a permanent release.
>
> If our request goes unanswered, we must examine the sincerity of our prayer. I believe this way of asking God to bring to mind the buried events of the past that we need to know in order to be free is a short cut to the long, tedious, and expensive process of psychoanalysis. Further than this, it brings the cure as well as the diagnosis.[2]

Stan scanned a number of pages before closing the book, then remarked, "Dr. Swain evidently understands Spiritual Laws, for he speaks of God as if he knowsHim. I notice that the sub-title of this book is, The Power Beyond Science. It is quite remarkable that he, a medical doctor and a man of science, should have such faith. Probably Dr. Swain talks of the power of faith as he treats his patients."

"Much of the book has references to such cases," I agreed.

"I notice that Dr. Swain states two things which he did. First he says that God will bring up from the unconscious whatever needs to be known." Stan looked at me searchingly and asked, "Have you found this to be true?"

"Many persons with whom I have shared in healing the memories have recalled incidents which took place far back of normal memory recall, even the traumas of birth sometimes have been relived. Nothing is hid from God, and the Holy Spirit brings seemingly forgotten

---

[2]From ARTHRITIS, MEDICINE AND THE SPIRITUAL LAWS by Loring T. Swain M.D. Copyright 1962 by Loring T. Swain. Reprinted by permission of the publisher, Chilton Book Company, Philadelphia.

experiences to memory, for it is the Holy Spirit who works on an individual's Subconscious Mind. "The Spirit searcheth all things, yea, even the deep things of God."[3]

Stan nodded, then said: "Doctor Swain also said he told his wife about the hurtful memory he had buried for forty years. Is it helpful to share such experiences in order to release them?"

"Sigmund Freud discovered the healing value of allowing his patient to talk of his troubles until they were all brought out into the open. It is interesting that God knew that a long time ago. James said to confess your faults one to another that you may be healed.[4] Paul advised his followers to bear one another's burdens.[5] We seem to need the support of one another for Jesus sent out his workers, not one alone, but two together. Talking freely with a friend who is trustworthy, who will keep secret all you say and whose reliance on God builds a bridge between yourselves and Him is helpful."

Stan looked at me searchingly, then smiled as he said, "I believe you qualify. Will you help me to recall the hurts of my past and to release them so that I shall not be over sensitive and feel as unworthy as I have all my life?"

"I shall stand by and pray to build a bridge," I answered.

---

[3]I Corinthians 2:10
[4]James 5:16
[5]Galations 6:2

12

Release the Child of Your Past

> AND HE WENT DOWN WITH THEM, AND CAME TO NAZARETH, AND WAS SUBJECT UNTO THEM.... AND JESUS INCREASED IN WISDOM AND STATURE, AND IN FAVOR WITH GOD AND MAN.
>
> Luke 2:51, 52 (KJ)

"How do we begin?" Stan asked.

"Relax, let go of every tension, put yourself into neutral and allow God to push you around," I answered.

"Ummm," Stan sighed as he settled into his chair.

"You may have experienced a hurt so early in life that you can not recall it. This may have become a hard-pan which blocks complete release. However, there is an all-knowing Mind back of the human mind which records all things. Allow yourself to merge into this Intelligence.

"Jesus said, 'The Spirit of the Lord is upon me, because he hath anointed me to preach the gospel to the poor; he hath sent me to heal the broken-hearted, to preach deliverance to the captives, and recovering of sight to the blind, to set at liberty them that are bruised,'[1] Many persons are made captive by fear and are bruised by traumatic experiences. Jesus can release these."

"Just how is it done?" Stan asked.

"Make of your mind a white screen on which incidents from your past may appear as scenes from a movie. Beginning with today allow the story of your life to roll backward.

"Relive each incident. Feel it as you felt it when it happened. When you feel some emotion, stop. The force of the emotional impact usually will indicate the intensity of feeling you had at that time. Feel as you felt this experience in actuality. Emotionally, you should be the child you were at the time of this experience. Say what you wanted to say at that time. Cry if you would have cried."

"What if I wanted to hit somebody?" Stan asked.

"Then get up and pound the stuffin' out of your chair cushion. Get the resentment out of your system. When freed from this you may be able to laugh. When you can laugh, you will be getting the upper hand of the situation."

"That would be something," Stan murmurred.

For some time Stan was quiet. Then he began talking in a monotone. Gradually his voice grew more positive. His body became tense as he relived conflicts with his brother. He became rigid as he relived whippings by his father whose stern demands inflamed rebellion.

Once Stan cried, "Dad didn't try to understand me. He never let me state my case!"

"It doesn't matter what another person has done," I protested. "You do not know what hurts he endured during his early life nor what caused him to act as he did. You must now release him to God who can take care of the situation better than you can. Paul wrote: 'Dearly beloved,

[1]Luke 4:18

avenge not yourselves, but rather give place unto wrath: for it is written, 'Vengeance is mine; I will repay, saith the Lord'.[2] If you want to hang onto your hurts and enjoy feeling abused, then don't expect God to do anything for you. God said he would remove our sins from us as far as the east is from the west,[3] but even God can't take a sin or a hurt from us unless we want to get rid of it, turn loose of it and let it go."

For a time Stan seemed relaxed as he sat quiet and limp.

Then, suddenly be began to cry. He buried his face in his hands and his shoulders shook convulsively under the flood of some remembered grief.

I waited quietly for the storm to pass.

At last, between sobs, Stan spoke. "You said that the most traumatic experience a child suffers is in being shut off from love."

"Yes."

"All my life I have felt there was a hardpan of hurt, deep within me, but I did not know what it was. I did not know until now when I saw it. The Spirit must have revealed it to me for I lived it all over again."

"Would you like to tell me about it?"

"Yes," Stan choked.

"Relax until you are more composed and can talk easily," I suggested, but Stan shook his head and went on.

"I was too young to remember, but I do recall hearing Mother say that I was a year and a half old at the time she was rushed to a hospital for serious surgery. I was left with a neighbor who lived down the street to be cared for during the day. There I was lonely and afraid. Father would fetch me after his work in the evenings. Al must

---

[2]Romans 12:19
[3]Psalm 103:12

have been with Uncle Frank and Aunt Alice on their farm that summer, for Dad and I were alone.

"He usually carried me to our house and as soon as I got there I would run from room to room looking for Mother. But night after night there was no mommie. The house was empty, the night filled with darkness. A great fear took hold of me that I never would see her again. I was too young to talk so as to make my feelings understood. I could only look for Mother and call her name as I grew more desolate and fearful.

Again great sobs shook Stan's shoulders.

"It is amazing that a child so young can think and feel so deeply." he sobbed.

Softly I spoke, "It is love we crave most and babies can die for lack of it."

Presently Stan resumed his story.

"One evening as we went home Dad said, "Mommie is home."

"My heart nearly burst for joy. As I ran into the house I heard her call to me. There she was on her bed. I began to climb up beside her, but Father came and lifted me away as he said 'You don't need his knees in your incision.' and he carried me from the room.

"He took me to the kitchen and set me in my highchair.

"Immediately I began to climb out, but he set me down and put a cloth around my body and tied it behind the chairback. I was a prisoner, scarcely able to move and unable to get to my source of love and comfort, my mother. I thought I was being punished. I did not know what for, but felt that I must be very bad to be punished so severely.

"Father gave me some supper. I ate a few bites but it soon came up. I was very sick. All night my fever rose. Father walked the floor with me in the back bedroom with the door closed, probably so that I would not disturb mother in the front bedroom. He did what he could to quiet me. I am sure now that he had no idea what caused me to be sick. He was doing what he thought was best for both mother and me."

Stan fell silent.

"Do you know, I believe that resentment toward my Father was born in me that night. We both might have felt it throughout the years that followed."

"That could have been," I agreed.

"Poor Dad," Stan caught his breath in a sob. "He was doing his best, but I did not know it then."

"Knowing it now should enable you to forgive him for his later treatment of you," I offered.

"I never could talk to him," Stan sighed. "We had little grounds for communication. How I wish I might have understood him better."

"All right," I spoke cheerfully trying to break the tension, "you have relived this experience as you remember it. Now live it as it might have been."

"Could it have been different?" Stan cried. "Now it is set, unchangeable."

"No, it can be changed, redeemed, even now," I answered.

Stan looked at me in amazement.

"Jesus said, 'Behold, I make all things new.' This may sound unbelievable, but the Divine Spirit is able to enter into the spirit of the child you were and change this hurtful experience." I smiled quietly.

"Oh, Aunt Gen, you are incredible. But I will go along with you."

"All right. Let's see if a better story will unfold on the screen of your mind. We shall ask God to take out the hurt and to put kindness in its place. Now live it all over again. Your Father takes you up the street toward your home. He tells you your mother is there. You are excited as you run into the house. You hear your mother call to you. All right so far?" I paused.

"Yes, go on."

"You run into your mother's room and see her on her bed. You want to get near her, to touch her and have her touch you, so you try to climb up beside her. Imagine that your father gives you a boost so that you are beside your mother."

There was a long period of stillness.

"No. I can't see Dad doing that," Stan finally said.

"Then allow Jesus to do it."

"What?" Stan exclaimed.

"God is ever present, you know, and Jesus was there even though you did not see him," I answered. "Be receptive. Let Jesus lift you onto the bed."

There followed a long silence, then Stan almost jumped from his chair.

"He did it! My God! He did it! Something actually lifted me onto that bed!"

"Now enjoy being there beside your mother," I said. "Feel her arm about you, see her smile, listen as she talks to you. Put your hand against her cheek. Cuddle down and rest in the security of the love you have longed for."

"Umm." This deep sigh must have come from the eighteen month old baby who had come home and found security. His days of loneliness, uncertainty and fear were past. The memory of those days was washed away. Love enfolded the child, yes and the man.

As I looked at the grown man in the chair, I saw that his body was relaxed and his face radiant with happiness. Tears ran down his cheeks and in the joy of the experience he was reliving he did not bother to wipe them away. He seemed to be living in another realm, perhaps the time when a happy baby knew the love his heart yearned for, a time which was more vital than the present day.

Quietly I moved away and left him with his memories. My heart was filled with gratitude that God's tender compassion can reach little children, even those who have grown tall, when they return to Him in confidence as a little child.

It seemed a long time before Stan returned to the common day. When he rose from his chair his face looked as if he had seen a vision. As he walked around the room he began talking in snatches of sentences, evidently to himself; "I wouldn't have believed such a thing could happen . . . but it did . . . There is a Power . . . a Power that is real . . . The Mind of God is more than a saying . . . I see now how the man was healed of war memories. The Sacrament became a bridge over which he could contact the Healing Presence . . . We need bridges . . . Contact must be made if change is to be made . . . Is this the way God removes our transgressions from us as far as the east is from the west? . . . Blots out the remembrance of them . . . This is a miracle of divine grace, for that which has been remains forever an unchangeable fact. Yet, from the memory of him who is forgiven the hurt is taken away, blotted out . . . Marvelous!"

Standing silently at a window the young clergyman might have been exerting his analytical mind to harmonize his experience with his theology. Silence filled the room. After a time I spoke quietly.

"The greatness of God is also manifest as He enables man to rise to a dimension which approaches that of Himself."

Stan turned quickly. "What do you mean?" he asked.

"To err is human, to forgive is divine," I said. "When man is able to forgive he is acting like God. The heart of the Lord's Prayer is: *forgive us as we forgive those who have hurt us*. Godlike forgiveness is to forget the offense and release the offender."

There was no response. After a time I went on, "Traumatic experiences seem to blot out from a person's memory all the happy times he might have known. I do not underestimate the hurt you suffered the night you were shut away from your mother, but would it not help to get this night into proper perspective with the days and nights that had gone before it?

"You had lived five hundred days and nights secure in the love of your mother before this unhappy experience," I said. "Try to recall the security of your mother's arms, of falling asleep on her breast. Imagine, if you can not remember, gentle hands caressing your body, a smiling face wakening happiness in you. Love that flows from a mother to her child is nourishing. Try to recall and relive the happy days of your infancy and bask in the warmth of love."

"I do feel that warmth", Stan nodded.

"Using your will, try to project this feeling of security down through the years that followed. Know that deep, deep in your inner being whatever happened to you after this you were secure in the love of your mother. In the first sustaining love of your life you knew the purest love, and knowing it you are able to comprehend the love of God."

Stan smiled, a yearning look in his eyes, "I touched Him as I relived this babyhood experience. I wish I might know Him as a living reality in Life's common day."

"Keep your heart open to Him, we are promised that He will be found of us when we seek Him with our whole heart."

Stan spoke softly, "Some day I hope to thank you for all you have done for me. Just now I must get away alone and think through all that has transpired today."

A smile, a wave of the hand and he was gone.

13

The Sins of the Fathers

...MOSES ROSE UP EARLY...AND WENT UP UNTO MOUNT SINAI, AS THE LORD HAD COMMANDED HIM, AND TOOK IN HIS HAND THE TWO TABLETS OF STONE.... AND THE LORD PASSED BY BEFORE HIM, AND PROCLAIMED, THE...LORD GOD, MERCIFUL AND GRACIOUS, LONGSUFFERING, AND ABUNDANT IN GOODNESS AND TRUTH, KEEPING MERCY FOR THOUSANDS, FORGIVING INIQUITY AND TRANSGRESSION AND SIN, AND THAT WILL BY NO MEANS CLEAR THE GUILTY; VISITING THE INIQUITY OF THE FATHERS UPON THE CHILDREN... UNTO THE THIRD AND TO THE FOURTH GENERATION.

Exodus 34:4, 6, 7 (KJ)

Who can know the depth of Divine Love or comprehend the reach of God's power? The Spirit continues to unfold truth overlooked in the writings of Scriptures. I stand in awe of the power of Christ Jesus to blot out the sins of this present time and of all times past, as is forshadowed by the ancient story in Exodus.

My friend Sara Reynolds was ill. This was most unusual for this young woman who had managed her life capably without the help of anyone. A university professor, efficient and poised, Sara did well in everything she undertook.

It might have been the shock of her father's death by suicide, soon after a large sum of money was discovered missing from the firm for which he worked, that brought on Sara's trouble.

She finished the spring term of school, then collapsed. For want of a better diagnosis, it was said she had a nervous breakdown. Sara sank into deep depression and withdrew from all association with people. As the days wore on, she gave way to fits of rage in which she screamed, threw anything at hand, tore up books and broke china. Such spells of violence usually ended in uncontrollable weeping. This was followed by a deep lethargy.

I had known Sara when she was a girl, for her mother was my friend, and later we had been associated in literary work. Mrs. Reynolds had called me during the past weeks, and each time I had gone to her home in an effort to help Sara. But so far, nothing had helped her. Now Mrs. Reynolds called again. The doctors who were caring for Sara were insisting that she be hospitalized and given shock treatments. As if grasping at a last straw, her mother pleaded, "Oh, please come again."

I talked the matter over with my husband and asked his advice.

"Unless something is done to help Sara soon, she will be in a mental institution," George said.

"There must be some avenue of God's Power that I have not found," I said. "It seems strange, but all summer as I have prayed for Sara, the story of the scape goat has kept coming to my mind."

"That may have significance," George said, looking at me intently. "Sin is back of most human suffering. It may be the sin of those who suffer or more probably the sins of persons who create the conditions which cause suffering. The scape goat afforded a release from the consciousness of the guilt of the Children of Israel as they wandered in the Wilderness. They were a primitive people, nomads who had long been slaves in Egypt, yet their basic needs were the same as ours today. They became distressed by the sense of guilt that weighed upon their minds, and carried the matter to Moses who took it to God. Moses was instructed to use a ceremony in which the people might lay their sins upon a goat. When this goat was driven into the wilderness away from the people they felt that their sins were taken away. This, as crude as it was, typified the full atonement for sins which was to come through Jesus Christ who was to take away the sins of the world."

"I see that this may have a bearing on Sara's condition," I agreed, "but recently I have been led to read again and again the scriptures which tell of the sins of the fathers being visited upon their children unto the third and fourth generation of them who hate God. This is not written once but time after time it is repeated. It is in Exodus 20:5, Exodus 34:7, Deuteronimy 5:9 and references are made to it in the Psalms and other writings of the prophets. This must have had great importance at the time it was written. These two scriptures must have some message concerning Sara's illness."

"I hope you find it," George added.

"It is an awful thought that the sins of forefathers as far back as the third and fourth generation might influence the lives of persons who are living today." I said. "Do you realize that the parents, grandparents, great grandparents and great-great grandparents of a person would total thirty individuals? Think what a cloud of witnesses, as Paul said, this would be. What sins unforgiven did they carry to their graves? What vibrations of hate, enmity, revenge, greed and other attitudes might they have released into the atmosphere when their spirits left this earth?"

"That is only speculation," George commented. "You are getting into deep water."

"Let us pray that wisdom shall be granted, and if there is a message here for Sara's healing that God will reveal it," I said. "I must pray. Will you join me in prayer that I shall be led aright?"

We sat together for perhaps half an hour, silently praying. At last I felt a great peace sweep over me and I felt God's answer would come. I thanked George for his fellowship of prayer and kissing his forehead bade him good night.

I went to bed, but not to sleep. Drifting into the area between sleep and waking I experienced what might be called a vision. I seemed to be standing alone in a quiet room. When I looked at the floor I saw a rope. Picking it up, I began to pull, only to find it was coming through a hole in the wall. Although it was frayed, dirty and greasy, I continued to draw it to me until it was a great pile there by my side.

Amazed and horrified I exlaimed, "What is this?"

"Sins," the answer came as if from a voice close beside me.

"Oh Lord!" I cried, "I never sinned that much."

As I waited I looked into the distance and saw Jesus kneeling in the Garden of Gethsemane. His shoulders were bowed and his head rested on his folded arms. There swept over me the awareness that it was here he took upon himself the sins of the world, not only the sins of people who were living at that time but all the sins that ever had been committed and ever shall be so long as time shall last, when the persons who have sinned carry their guilt and release it to him.

Again the voice spoke; "Carry these sins and lay them on the bowed shoulders of Jesus."

The thought was repulsive. I cried out, "Oh, my God,

I can't! I can't do such a thing to Jesus. He has suffered enough!"

As I wept, I seemed to hear a gentle voice from a distance saying, "For this cause came I unto the world."

This then, was the will of Christ. He bade me do it, so weeping, I gathered up the dirty rope and stumbling blindly made my way to the garden.

Jesus did not move as I approached. I stood still. Waiting, praying, then I laid the rope on his shoulders.

Exhausted, I dropped at his side. Fumbling blindly through my tears I touched his robe. I clutched it in my hand. A feeling of peace stole over me and healing flowed through my body. After a time I felt his hand gently drawing me to his side.

When I was drained of anguish and peace had flowed into me, I rose and stepped back. As I looked at Jesus I saw that the rope had been absorbed into his body. There remained on his shoulders only the print of the coiled rope like the form of a serpent.

I lay awake a long time. The Holy Presence was very close. I felt amazed at God's patience with my dull understanding. The answer I had sought for weeks was clearly printed in His Word, yet, He had used a vision to show it to me.

When I told George of this experience, he agreed it was the answer I had sought. So I went again to the Reynolds' home.

Sara was in a quiet mood and remained in the room as her mother and I visited. We included her in the conversation but she only looked away as if gazing into the distance and made no response.

"Sara," I said, turning my attention to her, "God has given me a message that is just for you. God loves you so much that He has shown me a great truth and has sent me to tell you about it."

"It is no use. I'm lost." Sara said flatly. "I have ruined my life." She turned her head as if to get away from me. "Guilt, guilt and sin weigh me down. I never can be free of them. It is hopeless."

Dejectedly Sara slumped in her chair.

"Oh, no, Sara, you have not sinned so greatly," I protested. "It may be that the shock of your father's death —"

I got no further, for Sara broke in, screaming, "My father! Don't you speak of my father. You didn't know what he was. People didn't know. They thought he was strong and forceful and successful. Efficient was the word used to describe him. Yes, he was those things, but only on the surface. His disgrace only showed the world what he was underneath his hypocritical exterior."

Jumping from her chair, Sara screamed, "We know! We of the family knew him all the time. He was mean and hard and vengeful. He broke everything that he could not bend to his will, even his children. I quailed before him when I was a child and the fear he instilled in me then hangs over me now. It is driving me crazy!" Sara's voice rose to a screech.

"Sara, listen," I tried to calm her, but she went on.

"He dominates me! I tell you he still dominates me! I can't get away from him. His genes are in my body. It is no use. He is stronger than I am. I can't shake him off."

Compassion flooded over me. Without premeditation I ran and put my hands on Sara's shoulders. She sank in her chair.

Dropping beside her I placed my hands on her knees. Mrs. Reynolds quietly slipped from the room.

"Listen Sara," I pleaded, "God loves you. God loves you so much that He has given me a message especially for you. God knows exactly how you feel. He wants to release you completely from the suffering you have endured."

Sara sat like a stone.

Looking intently into her face, I called her name, "Sara, Sara." When she looked at me I held her eyes with mine.

Gradually she relaxed. After awhile her face showed response.

Quietly I told her of the passages of Scripture that repeatedly had come to my mind as I prayed for her. I spoke of their meaning to the people who sought God long ago, and of God's provision for the forgiveness of sins, even then, and of the ultimate provision for forgiveness of sins through His Son, Christ Jesus.

Sara stared at me wonderingly. The stony look on her face changed. Her eyes widened. Finally she asked, "Could God help me?"

"God so loved the world that he gave his Son that whosoever believeth on him shall have life, life everlasting and life now." I quoted, "That whosoever means everyone."

"Even if they are dead?" Sara asked wonderingly.

"Whatever sins we lay on Jesus he assumes." I answered.

"Can Jesus take the sins of my father and remove their influence from over me so that I shall not be driven crazy?"

"He can," I declared firmly.

Sara was quiet for a time, then she shook her head.

"No." Sara withdrew into her shell, "I have to do it myself."

"Yes, my dear, you are so right," I patted her knee as I drew her attention. "So right," I repeated. "Only God can forgive sins but there are things that each of us must do to help Him. These things we must do ourselves."

"What?" the word was defiant.

"You must believe that God is, and is a rewarder of them that diligently seek Him.[3]

---

[3]Hebrews 11:6

"You must want to be forgiven and healed.

"You must realize that your attitudes of hate and resentment are sins.

"You must accept the sins of your fathers and grandfathers, as well as those of your grandmothers, as yours by heritage.

"You must lift them and take them to yourself.

"You must carry all of these, your own sins, and theirs, to Jesus.

"You must lay all of these upon him.

"There, you must release them and let them go completely."

I remained beside Sara as I looked intently into her face, searching her eyes. Presently she shifted position, then looked at me and spoke.

"I want," her voice faltered, "I want to go to the church."

My heart sang. I wanted to dance for joy. This was victorious. Now we were on our way to release and healing.

After telling Mrs. Reynolds where we were going, Sara and I went to my car. For some minutes we drove in silence, then Sara spoke hesitantly, "I did not want to say this before mother, but sometimes I feel there is a demon or evil spirit in me that makes me do the things I do."

My hands steadied on the steering wheel and I looked intently down the road. "I am told that when an unhappy idea is held for a long time and dwelt upon it may become an obsession.

"Thoughts bring forth things. Attitudes of criticism, faultfinding, hatred, resentment, self pity, jealousy and the like, long indulged in, may turn into an evil spirit of these things. We must guard our thoughts, for evil can enter by the doorway of our minds and emotions. When we give over our emotions to evil thoughts, the evil of those thoughts may take possession of us.

"Jesus recognized the reality of evil spirits and cast them out," I continued. "He gave his followers power to heal the sick and cast out devils.[4] To us who serve him today, he gives that power." [5]

"What is that power?" Sara asked.

"It is the power of the name of Jesus Christ. No evil thing can stand before that name. When you lay your burden of guilt on the shoulders of Jesus put the demon on the top of the pile. I shall command, in the name of Jesus Christ that it leave you."

"All right," Sara said simply.

Sara led the way into the church. We stood before a window which portrayed Jesus in the Garden of Gethsemane. Light glowing through the stained glass seemed to make the picture come alive. A sacred stillness enfolded us as we knelt before the altar. A light seemed to radiate from above. Presently the stillness was broken by a sob, then another which led to a torrent of tears. The weeping continued as if the very depth of Sara's being was broken up. I slipped my arm around her as she slumped over the rail and held her gently. It was evident that "the Spirit knoweth the deep things of the heart,"[6] and was doing His work.

After a time Sara rose and stood looking at the figure upon the cross above the altar. A smile played upon her lips. Her face was bathed in light. She straightened her shoulders, and arm in arm we walked down the aisle.

Sunshine bathed the world outside. We stood together in the open doorway, basking in its warmth. Sara threw back her shoulders and drew in deep breaths as if she were breathing the very breath of God.

Looking back into the narthex, I asked, "Is there a small

[4]Luke 9:1
[5]John 17:20
[6]I Corinthians 2:10, Romans 8:27

room off the vestibule where we might talk?"

"There is a little garden around here somewhere," Sara answered. "I used to go there to meditate, but I haven't seen it for a long time. Let's see if we can find it."

14

The Power and Protection of the Holy Spirit

BUT YE SHALL RECEIVE POWER. AFTER THAT THE HOLY GHOST IS COME UPON YOU: AND YE SHALL BE WITNESSES UNTO ME . . .

Acts 1:8

The garden was a delightful surprise, tucked in between the walls of the sanctuary and educational building, it was an oasis of green, welcoming wayfarers to rest and find peace. Grass carpeted the ground while tall shrubs banked the gray stone walls. Benches rested against the shrubs and in the center of the garden a statue of Saint Francis of Assisi stood among rose bushes covered with blossoms that perfumed the quiet air.

"It is just as I remember it," Sara breathed. "So few things remain the same."

"It is lovely" I agreed. "It is like the bishop's garden which he described as being narrow but very high. It is high, for the sky seems to bend low to become a part of it."

A smile lighted Sara's face. "I am glad you said that.

I used to feel the same way about the sky being a part of this garden. Maybe fairies dance here just before sunrise."

Was Sara speaking? I looked quickly to see if the speaker really was she. A transformation certainly had taken place to change the distressed woman who had come to this church an hour ago into the imaginative girl she once had been. Tears filled my eyes and I turned to the rose bed to hide them.

Now Sara was beside me. "I feel so happy, so free," she cried. "The crushing thing, that weighed upon me like a black blanket, has been lifted and the monkey has been taken off my back. Do you think they ever will come back?" Her voice held a note of terror. "I hope not! Oh, I hope not!"

"Let us sit down," I suggested moving toward a bench. "This is a perfect place to talk." As we walked together slowly, I prayed that God might give me the right words to speak to Sara.

"We are on a pilgrimage with Jesus," I began slowly. "First there was the journey to Jesus in the Garden of Gethsemane where you laid upon his shoulders all the sins of your ancestors. We knelt together at his cross as we knelt at the altar of this church. Now, in this garden, let us think of Jesus in another garden as he stood beside his empty tomb. He was the risen Christ who had conquered death, but his work was not yet finished. As Mary approached him, he said, 'Touch me not, for I am not yet ascended to my father.'[1] His mortal life was ended. If those who loved him ever were to touch him it must be a contact of their spirits with his.

"In their shock and grief, his followers had forgotten that Jesus had said, 'I will not leave you comfortless.'

---

[1]John 20:17

He had promised to send them another Comforter, 'even the Spirit of Truth; whom the world cannot receive because it seeth him not, neither knoweth him; but you know him; for he dwelleth with you, and shall be in you.' "[2]

Turning to Sara I asked, "Can you imagine how the disciples must have felt after Jesus was crucified?"

Sara sat thoughtfully meditating. She spoke with feeling, "They must have been bereft. Their hopes shattered, for they were alone, their leader gone. Fear must have gripped them."

"There must have been a great emptiness in their hearts," I went on. "Jesus planned to fill the empty places in their lives. They loved him, so they did as he told them, and waited ten days in the Upper Room at Jerusalem with prayer and supplication, until the fulfillment of his promise.

"The story in Acts reads: 'And when the day of Pentecost was fully come, they were all with one accord in one place. And suddenly there came a sound from heaven as of a rushing mighty wind, and it filled all the house where they were sitting. And there appeared unto them cloven tongues like as of fire, and it sat upon each of them. And they were all filled with the Holy Ghost, and began to speak with other tongues, as the Spirit gave them utterance.'[3] Then Peter stood up and preached to the throng of people from every surrounding country, telling of the resurrection of Jesus, and every man there heard in his own tongue."

"That was a miracle," Sara exclaimed. "And their changed lives were a miracle too. As I recall the story, they were a pretty sorry lot. Weak, vacillating, striving for position and one of them even denied he ever knew

---

[2]John 14:16-18
[3]Acts 2:1-4

Jesus. But after this they were invincible."

"Yes, it was said of them that they had turned the world upside down."

"But the Holy Spirit was in the world before Pentecost," Sara said. "In the first of Genesis when the earth was without form and void, it was the Spirit that moved over the waters and brought chaos into cosmos."

"And the prophets of old spoke as they were directed by the Spirit," I continued. "We are told that all scripture is given by inspiration of God.[4] The prophet Joel foretold a time when the Holy Spirit would be outpoured upon all people and all Christian believers might be filled with the Spirit as God's chosen few formerly had been. He said, 'And it shall come to pass . . . that I will pour out my Spirit upon all flesh; and your sons and your daughters shall prophesy, your old men shall dream dreams, and your young men shall see visions.'[5]

"On down through sacred history God's Spirit continued to be manifest. After Jesus was baptized by John in the river Jordan the Holy Spirit descended upon him in the form of a dove and the voice of God sanctioned his ministry, saying, 'This is my beloved Son, in whom I am well pleased.'[6]

"The Christian's experience of conversion is called the New Birth, and is an act of the Spirit, as Jesus told Nicodemus, "Except a man be born of water and of the Spirit, he cannot enter the kingdom of God. That which is born of the flesh is flesh; and that which is born of the Spirit is spirit.' "[7]

Sara looked up questioningly, "I often have wondered why the Holy Spirit came upon Jesus as a dove, yet it

---

[4]II Timothy 3:16
[5]Joel 2:28
[6]Matthew 3:17
[7]John 3:5-6

came upon the hundred and twenty in the Upper Room at Jerusalem as tongues of fire."

"Perhaps it was that fire purifies," I answered. "Humankind needs to be cleansed of their natural perversity. Jesus had no sin, so he needed no purifying fire. Besides cleansing, fire illuminates. The Holy Spirit cleanses, enlightens and imparts wisdom."

Sara leaned toward me smiling, a twinkle in her eyes, "Pardon me if I seem irreverent, but Jesus gave the Water of Life and the Holy Spirit sends fire. Fire and water generate power. Didn't Jesus say, 'you shall have power after the Holy Spirit is come upon you'?"

"He certainly did," I agreed. "Fire affords brightness. Christians should be a glowing people. Those who followed Christ were called Little Christs, perhaps because the glow of his spirit radiated from them. True Christianity always has imparted a glow to human lives. Quakers speak of the Burning Heart, John Wesley, founder of the Methodist Church, felt his heart strangely warmed as he knelt in a little chapel in London. The experience of the Warm Heart was the motivating power of this church in its early growth."

"Seems like the Church has kind'a slipped, doesn't it?" Sara smiled.

"Let us trust that the Church is still the Body of Christ," I said.

Sara sat quietly meditating for some minutes, then turning toward me she asked, "How is the Holy Spirit manifest?"

"He is called the Comforter, which may mean one who gives comfort, for God said long ago, 'as one whom his mother comforteth, so will I comfort you,'[8] but a better description would be one who comes to help or assist."

Sara looked up quickly. "If translated from the Latin,

[8]Isaiah 66:13

the word comfort might be *com forte,* which means with strength or power."

"It is good to be with a person who knows her Latin," I patted Sara's knee as I smiled, then went on, "The Holy Spirit is teacher.[9] He bears witness to Jesus and brings to remembrance the things Jesus said.[10] He makes intercession for us,[11] as one who loves a friend might intercede. He is the spirit of truth,[12] and the Spirit itself beareth witness with our spirit, that we are children of God."[13]

In a lighter vein I said, "Some radio stations conduct a Swap Shop which affords opportunity for persons to exchange things they do not need for useful articles. God has such a Swap Shop. Long ago He proclaimed that He would give beauty for ashes, the oil of joy for mourning, the garment of praise for the spirit of heaviness.[14] Think how joyous it would be to take to God the burned out ashes of our failures, disappointments and hurts and receiving in exchange for them His gift of Beauty! To carry to Him our grief and mourning and have our hurt places anointed with the healing Oil of Joy! What a relief is in store for us when we allow Him to take from our shoulders the Spirit of Heaviness that depresses us and give us in its place a Garment of Praise!

"You may not realize now that you have an empty place in your life, but if you try to live without giving God an opportunity to fill the place from which your guilt and depression were removed, they may return."

"Like the house Jesus spoke of from which an evil spirit was cast out, but to which the evil thing returned with

[9]John 14:26
[10]John 14:26
[11]Romans 8:26
[12]John 16:13
[13]Romans 8:16
[14]Isaiah 61:3

several more of his kind and filled the house," Sara said. "I certainly wouldn't want that."

"Many persons who have received healing or release from mental distress and think only of getting well while giving no attention to developing their spiritual life, find their sickness returning to them. They should remember the words which Jesus spoke to one whom he healed when he said; 'Sin no more, lest a worse thing come upon you.' "[15]

"It might help if we have the Fruits of the Spirit," Sara said.

"What is the difference between the fruits of the Spirit and the gifts of the Spirit, as Paul wrote about them?"

"As fruits that grow on trees and vines are produced by the sap that rises from the roots into the branches, so the Holy Spirit within the life of the dedicated Christian brings forth in him the characteristics known as the Fruits of the Spirit. These are: love, joy, peace, longsuffering, gentleness, goodness, faith, meakness and temperance, or patience.[16] These abound in us according to the degree in which the Holy Spirit possesses our lives.

"The Gifts of the Spirit are resident in the Spirit, and are evidenced in the lives of Spirit filled Christians to edify the believer and glorify God. These are: the word of wisdom, the word of knowledge, faith, gifts of healings, working of miracles prophecy, discerning of spirits diverse kinds of tongues and interpretation of tongues.[17]

"After listing these gifts, Paul concluded his chapter by saying: 'Covet earnestly the best gifts; and yet I show unto you a more excellent way.' He then wrote the magnificent Love Chapter, of First Corinthians, thirteen. In this

---

[15]John 5:14
[16]Galatians 5:22,23
[17]I Corinthians 12:8, 9, 10

he says that love exceeds all other gifts of the Spirit and will abide when they have passed away. Love is eternal, for God is Love, and the Holy Spirit is Divine Love in Action."

"Divine Love in Action," Sara looked at me wonderingly. "The Holy Spirit is Divine Love in Action. Oh, that is beautiful!"

Sara's body relaxed as if dropping a heavy load. She threw back her head and laughed softly. "This is wonderful. I've been afraid of receiving the Holy Spirit, afraid I would become fanatical or odd. But the Spirit is truly Divine Love in greater abundance than I have known. Right?"

"Right," I smiled.

Sara caught her breath, her eyes alight. "I'm beginning to see the meaning of the Trinity. How do you understand this great truth?"

"Once when I was praying to understand this profound mystery, this came to me," I said, holding up my left hand. "I have five fingers," I went on, "each is individual, complete and separate, yet all join as one in my palm, constituting a hand. The work of the hand is largely done by the fingers, while their action is directed by the mind that motivates them. The fingers of an organist produce music, yet his trained mind directs his fingers.

"The three Persons of the Trinity, Father, Son and Holy Spirit each is complete in Himself, yet all are One, each acting to reveal God as the Divine Mind directs them. They are individual in action, yet one in Mind and purpose.

"Each Person of the Trinity bears witness of the others. The Holy Spirit bears witness of Jesus. He told His disciples, 'I have yet many things to say unto you, but you cannot bear them now. Howbeit when he, the Spirit of Truth, is come, he will guide you into all truth; for he shall not speak of himself; but whatsoever he shall hear, that shall he speak: and he will show you things to come. He shall glorify me: for he shall receive of mine, and shall show it unto you.'[18]

"Jesus spoke in the same way about his relationship with His Father. He said, 'The Son can do nothing of himself, but what he seeth the Father do . . . these also doeth the Son likewise.'"[19]

Sara was leaning forward, a look of contemplation on her face. "Then the Holy Trinity is One in Mind and Spirit, three as they each reveal God to man."

"Yes," I agreed, "The Holy Spirit continued the work Jesus began, but has greater power, being everpresent Spirit, Jesus could talk to those who heard his voice, but the Spirit knows the thoughts of every heart, everywhere. The Spirit can be with every person in the world at the same time. Since the Holy Spirit comes to abide in the lives of Christians, it is He who acts within us as a guide and leader. He corrects, cleanses, strengthens and directs our lives in channels of useful service for God's Kingdom."

"The same Spirit that was in Jesus." Sara repeated, "I love that thought. The Holy Spirit is not a strange, frightening power that takes possession of people, but He is the Christ Spirit that was in Jesus, magnified by Infinity. He is loving, gentle, healing, binding up hurts and wounds."

"Yes," I agreed, "Strengthening, protecting, imparting wisdom and power, as those who receive Him are capable of receiving it. You might fill your cup at the beach but your cup could not contain the ocean. You might have of the water of the ocean, true, but never possess all the water there. We may receive the Holy Spirit to the fullness

[18]John 16:12-14
[19]John 5:19

of our capacity, yet it is the height of human arrogance for persons who have been blessed by receiving the Holy Spirit to say that they 'have it all'.

"The baptism by the Holy Spirit is a definite experience following conversion," Sara reinterated.

"Jesus told those who had learned of him for three years, to wait for it. So, we condition our lives to receive it today. Jesus said it was necessary to die to self in order to live unto God. He calls us to total commitment to God.

Sara looked up. "Will you pray that I receive the Holy Spirit?"

Compassion flooded over me. "My dear, understand with your deepest knowing that your Father God and the gentle heart of the Holy Spirit are longing to take possession of your life. Give Him your will, your emotions, your abilities, great and small, Give yourself to Him. Hold nothing back. Expect. Receive Him. Jesus said the Father would give the Holy Spirit to them that asked Him, even as an earthly father would give good gifts to his children.[21] Open your heart to Him and ask the Holy Spirit to come in."

Sara was relaxed, expectant. God had done so much for her this day that she was ready to believe Him capable of anything.

Soon a light came over her face. She lifted her head and began to laugh. The laughter continued until ripples of holy laughter filled the garden. Unmindful of anything except of the Spirit that filled her, Sara rose and walked about the garden, praising and adoring God as she thanked Him for His wondrous mercy.

Returning to me, Sara said with voice filled with joy, "He has come! He has come and filled me with love to overflowing."

---

[21]Luke 11:13

Grasping my hand and holding it tightly Sara turned tear filled eyes to mine. In a voice touched with awe and wonder she said, "Everyone should have an empty place, so that God could fill it with His love."

"Everyone does have an empty place," I said, "It is a place the Creator reserved for Himself, but man has filled it with his Ego-Centric-Self, as he tries to be God. This was the first temptation to which mankind ceded. Satan's temptation was, 'Eat this, and you shall be as God', and man has been trying to usurp the place of God and make a god of himself ever since. The pages of history are bloody with crimes of would-be-gods who have tried to conquer the world. Mad with their thirst for power they have led nations to disaster. Still they rise. Still men follow them while the Eternal God calls us to Himself.

"God cannot fill the place He designed for Himself in the life of man until this false god of Self is dethroned. This is the dying to self which is necessary before the Holy Spirit can fill the life of any individual.

"Except a grain of wheat fall into the ground and die —" Sara offered.

"Dying to self is a real death," I agreed. "The Ego cries out, *I* want to be important, *I* want the chief seat at the head table, *I* want to be chairman of the committee, *I* want to be the main speaker, I want to lead the band, *I* want to be *The Big It* on every occasion. It is this human *I* that is not subject to God, neither indeed can be."

"Is this why so many people fight against the baptism with the Holy Spirit?" Sara asked.

"Could be."

As Sara and I drove toward her home we were relaxed and happy.

"You should find a group of Christian friends with whom you can pray and share experiences," I said, thinking of the days ahead of Sara. "Fellowship is vital to human happiness. You know how a bed of coals in a fireplace glow as they are close together, but lift one coal out onto the hearth alone and it soon loses its luster and turns black.

"Many persons find the Bible hard to read, but the Spirit sheds light upon the Word. Read the Gospels until Jesus becomes real to you. Memorize his words. Allow his attitudes to motivate your actions. The Life of the Spirit is a walk with the most lovely Person who ever lived. Never separate the Holy Spirit from Jesus. While the Spirit gives us power, Jesus ever remains our pattern. Love Him, adore Him and emulate Him. He will give you his joy and lead you into glorious victory."

Sara resumed her teaching with her usual efficiency but those who knew her recognized a sweetness she never had possessed before.

15

Light Shines Through Clean Windows

SERVE THE LORD WITH GLADNESS: COME BEFORE HIS PRESENCE WITH SINGING.... ENTER INTO HIS GATES WITH THANKSGIVING, AND INTO HIS COURTS WITH PRAISE. ...FOR THE LORD IS GOOD; HIS MERCY IS EVERLASTING; AND HIS TRUTH ENDURETH TO ALL GENERATIONS.

Psalm 100:2, 4, 5 (KJ)

An atmosphere of peace and reverence pervaded the sanctuary as strains of organ music rose in prelude to the morning worship service. About me a number of ladies of the Tuesday morning prayer group sat in meditative silence and I knew they were visualizing the Light of God's Presence in His Holy Temple, as they had been doing for a number of weeks.

As the pastor stood before his congregation he gave evidence of his calling as a Minister of Jesus Christ. I might assume the role of a mother figure when he was in my home, but as the Reverend Mister Stanley Houston stood behind the pulpit, faced the altar, or administered the elements of the Holy Communion, he was my pastor,

God's ordained minister, set aside for His service. This I felt today, as I always had felt it when my husband ministered to his congregation.

My memory flashed back over the past spring and summer, during which time the young man before me had come into a consciousness of his true relationship with God. I rejoiced as I thought of his last talk with me.

Stan had returned from a visit with his brother. He had gone with Albert on a camping trip into a woods beside a river. There they had been alone, boating and fishing, cooking fish over an open fire, tramping, relaxing and talking together until they had come to know each other and to understand their mutual problems.

"I tried to explain to Al all you had told me about releasing past experiences and of healing the memories," Stan said. "That which I did not make clear one day, I tried to the next."

"How did Albert take it?" I asked.

"He was quite responsive," Stan answered. "I went with the determination to ask his pardon for my feelings of resentment toward him, but when I asked him to forgive me, he interrupted me, saying he had more reason to beg forgiveness than I. We talked over childhood experiences and cleared away all grievances between ourselves. Then we carried our father to the Throne of Grace, so to speak. I don't know that this did Dad any good, but it certainly helped us."

"You were acting in harmony with New Testament Christians," I said.

Stan eyed me questioningly as he asked, "What do you mean?"

"The Corinthian Christians did much the same thing when they observed the rite of baptism for their dead," I answered.

"Where do you get that?" Stan asked.

"In his first Letter to the Corinthian Church, after Paul had written at length about the resurrection of the dead, he said in the fifteenth chapter, the twenty ninth verse, 'Else what shall they do which are baptized for the dead, if the dead rise not at all? Why are they then baptized for the dead?' "

"I never read that," Stan commented, "At least it never registered in my mind."

"The baptism of John was for the remission of sins," I pointed out, "And if these early Christians found it helpful to be baptized for their beloved dead, and Paul approved the practice, why shouldn't we find it helpful to pray for ours?"

"So right," Stan nodded. "Anyway it seemed right that Al and I should lift our Father in love and prayer. Remembering the ills he endured during his childhood and youth, I felt a great peace after we had done this. It might have been the release within my own Consciousness, as I fully forgave him, but I would be happy to know that he also was blessed."

"What change has there been in your relationship with Lee?" I asked.

Stan laughed softly. "You know, that animosity literally dissolved when there was no feeling in me to respond to his. I had a frank talk with Lee, in which I made clear his duties and the limits of his responsibilities. He responded with a respect he had not shown before. Now we are getting along very well. Beth and Ann have been warm friends ever since we came here, so now the four of us have had some cook outs and little trips together. Life has been good since the experience of healing my childhood memories."

"Would you mind telling me of that experience?" I asked.

Stan smiled reminiscently, "The most wonderful thing

that came to me that day was a consciousness of the reality of God. His Spirit truly bore witness with my spirit when I released all hurts and resentments to Him, and let go all striving to be more than I am capable of being. I have hated weakness and wanted desperately to be strong, perhaps because I often had felt inadequate. This may have been why I sought intellectual achievement."

Stan hesitated some moments, then continued, "It seemed to me that God hated weakness. I thrilled to the words spoken to Saul as he lay stricken to the ground by the light from heaven while he was on his way to Damascus. The clarion words were, 'Rise, and stand upon thy feet: for I have appeared unto thee for this purpose, to make thee a minister and a witness.'[1] Then there is Paul's admonition to the Corinthian brethren to 'Watch ye, stand fast in the faith, quit ye like men, be strong.'"[2]

Stan smiled unsteadily, "I wanted above all things to be strong, yet there was something inside of me as quavering as jelly. That day on your terrace I gave God my pretense of strength and threw myself on His mercy, with all my weakness, my struggling and trying to keep up a front that I knew was not genuine. I realized there was in me much of the child which evidently cowered in my Deep Mind. So I lifted my weakness to Him as I begged His Spirit to redeem the child I once had been.

"As this was done something tremendous happened that revolutionized my understanding of myself. I suddenly realized that the child is necessary to the man. Knowing this gives humility to the mighty. Paul said that when he was a child he spoke and understood as a child. This was part of his development, which, when fulfilled, enabled him when he became a man, to put away childish

---

[1]Acts 26:16

[2]I Corinthians 16:13

things.[1] The child must precede the man, receptivity and trust go before knowledge and wisdom, for Jesus said it was necessary to become as a child in order to enter the Kingdom of Heaven.

"It came to me that when the child life of an individual is complete and fulfilled, leaving no deep traumas to hinder his growth, this person should develop into normal maturity. Paul deplored the necessity of feeding certain Christians on milk as if they were babes, because they were so underdeveloped that they could not digest the spiritual meat of the Word.[2]

"It was good that I felt humbled and gave God all of myself, even all my weakness. I trust that since He has lifted me up I shall be able to become the man He wants me to be."

Listening to Stan, I realized the depth of this man's character.

"Stanley, you accepted the experiment of Healing the Memories which I presented to you, but you have carried it into a higher dimension that I dreamed was possible. You are my teacher. I am awed and grateful for what you have shown me."

"Oh, Aunt Gen, you humble me. You have taught me much. Truly, I am grateful for all I have been through. We learn best by living, I suppose, that is, if we honestly do our best. I shall be better able to understand people who carry heavy loads, and able to have compassion for those who suffer, as I could not have done if I myself never had known a hurt. I shall mature to the stature of a strong man, able to stand on my feet before Him."

"I drove to the country after I left you," Stan continued, "And walked alone on the hills. There, I seemed to be

[1]I Corinthians 13:11

[2]I Corinthians 3:2

uplifted and filled with a great peace. I was like the aviator who felt he could reach out and touch the face of God. As I praised Him I seemed to grow lighter as if rising into a new dimension, or experiencing a new birth, as Jesus expressed it to Nicodemus. A new birth may come when a person relinquishes all of himself to God. This may be through the dying to self Jesus spoke of. It may be that we never experience this until we plumb the depth of our own lives, see all that is there, the tendency toward error and the possibility for good."

The music of the opening hymn brought my thoughts back to the worship service. There was a light on the minister's face as he arose and announced his text from Second Timothy, the first Chapter, and the Seventh Verse: 'For God hath not given us the spirit of fear; but of power, and of love, and of a sound mind.'

16

The Value of Dreams and Creative Thinking

NOW FAITH IS THE SUBSTANCE OF THINGS HOPED FOR, THE EVIDENCE OF THINGS NOT SEEN.
Hebrews 11:1 :1

WHERE THERE IS NO VISION, THE PEOPLE PERISH....
Proverbs 29:18 18

Thoughts, how important they are. On the looms of thought our dreams are spun and dreams design the fabric of our lives. So I mused as I drove over rolling hills and thought of the transformation dreams and hard work have made of this prairie land. It must have been dreams of homes that inspired the pioneers to come here.

I smiled as I recalled the story of Aunt Debby who stood upon a knoll of grass-covered prairie which she and her husband had staked out as their claim, and built aircastles of what was to be.

"There, Walt, on that knoll, we will build our house. A two storied house with green shutters. It will have a white picket fence with red hollyhocks and blue larkspur against the fence. To the north we will have our orchard with apples, and pears, and plums, and peaches, and apricots. We will plant alfalfa south of the house so that when the south wind blows we can smell alfalfa blossoms."

"It's all right to dream," Walt grumbled, "but it will be a sod house for now."

"But Walt, one has to dream." Debby protested. "If you are going to have a house you have to dream a house. And if you want an orchard you need to dream an orchard."

It may be that Aunt Debby's dreams enabled her to hang on to her hopes as winds blew about the little soddie and snow covered the prairie. It was a long time before the white house with its green shutters became a reality. But an orchard was planted and grew north of the house and south winds did carry fragrance of alfalfa as it blew over the blossoming field. Red hollyhocks and blue larkspur appeared along the white picket fence, an assurance, perhaps, which gave stability to Aunt Debby's dreams.

Through dreams we are able to visualize that which we hope for as though it were already attained. Conversely, we can recall happy experiences and relate them to the present, infusing the joy and beauty we have felt and known into the dullness of a dreary day. These thoughts ran through my mind as I drove home. As I hung up my coat I saw Stan at the front door.

"Oh, I'm tired." He moaned. "Two funerals today. I'm drained." His shoulders drooped and his face seemed drawn.

"I knew the Robert's funerals would be exhausting and I felt for you." I said.

"I must be in shape for the meeting tonight. It is very important." Stan glanced at his watch. "How can I make the necessary mental adjustment in a little more than two hours?"

"Does Beth know you are here?" I asked.

"No, I came directly from the cemetery."

"I will call her and ask her to hold dinner until you get home, and to allow no interruptions while you are eating." I said. "Take the lounge chair and relax."

When I returned to the room, Stan was moving restlessly, rubbing his hand over his eyes. "I can't get those crying children off my mind." he moaned, "They are so bereaved and alone."

"I understand how a pastor enters into the suffering of his people. I have seen my husband share such grief. You will visit those children in a few days and do all you can to help them adjust to life as they must face it, but now you must stop thinking about them. Release them to God's care. For the next hour you must relax."

"How?"

"By the proper direction of your wonderful mind." I answered. "Paul said, 'Be ye transformed by the renewing of your mind,' (Romans 12:2) This power is yours, it is waiting for you to use it. As you relax think of a small child as he lies asleep. See how limp his body is. Let yours be just as limp. Drop your hands, stretch your legs, now let them rest. Tense your neck, then let your head rest as if it does not belong to you. Visualize a soft light flooding your being. This is the light of life, allow it to renew your mind and body. Feel it as it warms your head, bringing new life to your brain, your thinking. It stimulates your eyes, your sinuses, your ears, it relaxes your throat. It renews life within you as you fill your lungs with oxygen. It makes you feel renewed as it touches your heart and speeds life giving blood to energize every fiber of your body. This light floods all the organs of your body, relaxing, renewing, restoring health. It touches your feet and hands, as it passes through your limbs. Be still, rest as the Light of Life renews you."

After a time of quietness, I said, "Think of the most

beautiful place you ever were in. Take yourself there again in thought. This might have been beside a mountain lake, on rolling prairie, beside a flowing river, or in a cool woods. Wherever it was, go back there in memory and relive the feeling you had as your enjoyed that particular moment of beauty.

"You and Beth vacationed in the Canadian Rockies. Close your eyes and be there again in memory. Sit beside Lake Louise and look across the emerald waters. See the mountains reflected on its mirror surface . . . feel the ecstasy of your first moment there . . . relive that feeling, give yourself to it . . . breathe its pure delight . . . feel peace, peace, peace."

I sat quietly watching the tension go out of the young man's face. I knew that his mental self was not in that chair. His body was there but his memory had taken him to some retreat which had brought him peace. The stress was going out of his limbs, his hands lay limp and his breathing was light.

"Now, think of a time when you felt some great happiness, some joy that was uplifting. Live that feeling over again."

Again stillness filled the room. Outside a bird broke into song. A cool breeze blew in carrying fragrance of freshly mown grass. The clock in the living room chimed. The young man lay still.

I picked up a pen and began making notes. Some minutes later Stan stirred. "How did you learn to do this," he murmured.

"If Wordsworth could see daffodils 'fluttering and dancing in the breeze' one summer day, then in winter when on his couch he lay, see them flash upon that inward eye, which is the bliss of solitude, we can do the same thing." I answered.

"Go on." Came the entreaty as I paused.

Perhaps my voice helped him to relax so I talked on softly.

"It is important that mental pictures be clear if we are to recall them with enjoyment. First impressions are lasting. When traveling, I try to reach important places when the light is best for viewing. I have seen the Grand Canyon many times, but I never shall forget the first time I saw it. Leaving the crowd around the Inn and driving to a place where the canyon gaps, an abyss of jagged rocks for four miles, I sank on the warm ground, mute with awe and wonder.

"How many millions of years had it been since the surface of earth cooled and its mountains pushed up? We are accustomed to mountains, but here was the opposite — a fissure in the crust of the earth. What had caused the rocks to break apart making this gigantic gorge? I felt infinitesimally small — a mere speck beneath the vast blue dome above. Stillness, so vast, so encompassing closed in that I felt lost in it, carried away by the pulse of time. 'What is man that Thou are mindful of him?' I breathed, as I sank lower on the grass and grew still, calm inside. Then, from somewhere, like music carried by the wind, a refrain sang in my mind: 'Thou hast made him a little lower than the angels and crowned him with glory and honor.'

"I sat up. The sun was lowering at the far end of the canyon. Shadows, blue, mauve and purple had crept into the depth of the gorge turning its rough interior into a symphony of colors, and the transformation had come through — shadows! Could the shadows of life transform man's haughty self-sufficiency into tolerance, forbearance and kindness?"

Stan was so still he seemed asleep. After a pause I softly said, "When George and I started for Mount Rushmore, I put some papers and a book of poems in my bag. We reached the mountain when the crowd of sightseers was milling about the refreshment stand. They were talking, yelling, eating, drinking, and taking pictures in a frenzy of haste to "do" as many places as possible on their vacation.

"We left, and got a cabin in view of the mountain. That evening we sat in the darkness while powerful lights played on the stone faces hewn in the granite mountainside, illuminating them against the black curtain of night. Early the next morning we returned to the mountainside. The ground below was strewn with soft drink bottles, cups, gum wrappers and cigarette packs. We climbed up the hillside where we could be alone and sat under a tree where the faces might look at us. Here we reviewed our country's history, recalling the soldiers of the Revolution who furnished their own guns and ammunition and went scantily clothed, even suffering from the cold as they defended this, their land. We talked of Washington, his sterling character and devotion to the cause of his country. We read some tributes to Jefferson, and to Teddy Roosevelt, then we talked of Lincoln's unexplainable greatness. I opened my book and read Edwin Markham's poem, Lincoln — The Man of the People. We felt the meaning of:

A man to meet the mortal need . . . .
Clay warm yet with the genial heat of Earth
That tender, tragic, ever-changing face; . . .
A man to match the mountains and the sea.

We had seen Mount Rushmore with our physical eyes but more than that we had glimpsed a deeper beauty with our inner eyes.

"It is good for us to understand the value of right thinking and to know what power our thoughts have. Dreams and creative imagination do much to form the pattern of our lives. Constructive thinking can help to establish our Christian faith. When our faith goes no deeper than the level of our Conscious Mind it may desert us when we need it most; when we are under pressure, off our guard or in times of distress. But when our faith is firmly established in our Deep Mind, which the Bible calls the heart or spirit, our faith will sustain us in times of trial and emergencies because it is then woven into the fiber of our innermost being.

"By Contemplative Meditation we establish in our Deep Minds the thoughts we repeatedly drop there. Now that you are relaxed, drop some solid stones into the well of your inner being to form a foundtion for your faith. Select that quality of life you desire to develop. Let us say that today it is Peace. Hold the thought, *peace,* in your mind, consider its meaning, its value, its blessings. Peace, peace, peace, roll the words over your tongue, instill their meaning in your heart until you become peace.

"Make a mental picture of some place of beauty you have enjoyed and put yourself in the center of this picture. Feel again the relaxation you knew as you shared the happiness of your honeymoon with Beth beside Lake Louise. Sit beside her again in memory and look out across those blue-green waters. Lift your eyes to the mountains which rise back of the lake, See the snow-capped summits. Drink in the beauty of color; the blue of the sky, the soft purple mountains darkening at their base, the rippling waters, See the lush green grass of the lawn around the Inn where you stayed. Feel the crisp, bracing air, clean , invigorating. Here you were alive, vibrant with happiness. The world was beautiful, life lay before you two who anticipated great things as you went forward together.

"The world is still beautiful. Your beloved stands beside you. There are great things to be done. They are awaiting you." I continued.

Stillness filled the room.

The man in the chair who seemed to be asleep turned his head and smiled. Stretching his arms he sat up, then was on his feet.

"What do I owe you for the treatment?" he grinned.

"See that it carries over into the evening." I said.

"Where is Uncle George? I want to thank him for allowing me to absorb so much of your time. He is a generous man to put up with me."

17

Jesus Is a Living Reality

THEN SHALL THY LIGHT BREAK FORTH AS THE MORNING, AND THINE HEALTH SHALL SPRING FORTH SPEEDILY: AND THY RIGHTEOUSNESS SHALL GO BEFORE THEE; THE GLORY OF THE LORD SHALL BE THEIR REWARD. THEN SHALT THOU CALL, AND THE LORD SHALL ANSWER; THOU SHALT CRY, AND HE SHALL SAY, HERE I AM.

Isaiah 58:8, 9

The telephone's ringing awakened me from a sound sleep. The voice over the wire was quavering with emotion. I listened, trying to get the story clearly. My head began to spin. I reached for the door casing to steady myself. When the phone was in its cradle I went to the front door, opened it and drew in deep breaths of the cool air. The clock pointed to half past three. I went back to the bedroom and shook George.

"What is it?" he mumbled.

"There's been a bad accident."

"Huh?" George sat up. "Who was it?"

"Lee and Ann."

"Anybody killed?"

"No. Both were badly hurt, Lee very seriously."

"Where did it happen?"

"East of town. They were coming home from the football game."

"Late to be getting home, isn't it?" George looked at the clock on the highboy.

"They and the Hustons' took dinner with friends in the city and spent the evening there," I said getting into my clothes. "It's a hundred and fifty mile drive back from the city. Come with me, we must go to the hospital."

"Were Stan and Beth hurt?" George asked, beginning to dress.

"No. They were in their car back of the Masters' car, when a drunken driver tried to pass a truck on a hill. He crashed into Lee's car. He wasn't even hurt but his car was demolished. Beth drove to the nearest house and phoned for the doctor and ambulance. Stan rode in the ambulance with Lee and Ann, and Beth drove in alone."

Silently we drove to the hospital. The night was clear and still. Few cars were on the streets at this hour. Softly we walked through the hospital, mindful of sleeping patients. Beth was standing outside the operating room and came down the corridor to us.

"Oh, it was awful," she choked.

I held her and patted her shoulder gently.

"They've just taken Ann to a room. The bones set nicely, they said. She is still under anesthesia. A nurse is with her."

"Where is Stan?" George asked.

"In there with Lee." Beth nodded toward the operating room. "He wouldn't leave Lee. They are so afraid Lee won't live." Beth began to sob.

Here, outside the operating room, the air seemed charged with suspense and oppressive with apprehension. What was going on behind those doors. Doctors were working to save a man's life, but was the man still breathing?

Waiting here, the worst could be imagined.

At this moment a thought came to me. Surgeons generally agree that persons in an operating room should be careful what they say for although the patient is completely anesthetized he still can hear. This seems to be an accepted belief by surgeons now.

My mind raced on. How could a person hear if he were completely "out" as the doctor said? Did his unconscious mind hear even while his conscious mind could hear nothing? It is an accepted fact that the deep mind governs the functions of the body. Is it also true that the deep mind can hear what is going on about one whose conscious mind is unable to hear and that words carelessly spoken may cause the body to respond to them. What a possibility to implant thoughts of health in the minds of the sick!

"I'm going to talk to the nurses," George said.

"Let's go to the Prayer Room," I said to Beth, "We can sit there and get our poise."

"I must be where Stan can find me," Beth protested.

"George will tell him where we are." I assured her, taking her arm.

In the prayer room we switched on the light above the picture of Jesus and sat in its soft glow.

"Lee looked so terrible when they dragged him out of that smashed car," Beth choked. "I can see him like that every time I shut my eyes — all covered with blood."

"Let's not think of him like that," I said. "See him as he was when you left the football stadium. He was happy and full of life then, wasn't he?"

---

[1]"'Surgeons and nurses must be careful of what they say even when the patient is anesthetized', said San Francisco's Dr. David B. Cheek. 'Even when the patient seems completely "out" he still can hear and may remember disturbing or embarrassing indiscretions'." TIME, February 8, 1960.

"Oh, yes," Beth looked up. "It had been such a perfect day, bright and sunny. We sat together and laughed a lot. We'd won the game and everybody around us was hilarious with happiness. Then we had such a good time at the Wagners. They are such fun and we hadn't been with them for a long time. We stayed later than we should have. Maybe if we had started home earlier we wouldn't have had this accident." Beth was shaking as in a chill and began sobbing.

"We can always think that we might have done differently." I said. "Right now let's do some helpful thinking and ask God to use it as our prayer."

"What shall we do?" Beth dabbed at her eyes and drew a choking breath that was half sob. She was shaking convulsively, I must help her. This was going further out than accepted thinking, but I would try it.

"We are told to 'let this mind be in you, which is also in Christ Jesus.'[1] Let us ask God that the calmness of the mind of Christ will now come into us. When we have this calmness let's pray that the strength which is in us through God's presence may be in Lee. He needs strength now. Let's breathe evenly, smoothly, drawing in the breath of life and know that the word which is translated "breath" in the New Testament is also translated "spirit". So, as we breathe we shall pray that the spirit of God — of life — shall sustain Lee."

"I'll try," Beth sobbed.

So we began our deep breathing prayer. Peace pervaded the room. Soon Beth was asleep, her head on the chairback against my coat. I do not know how long we were in the Prayer Room, but it must have been exactly the right time for when Beth awoke and we went again to the operating room Stan was coming out.

---

[1]Phil. 2:5

"How's Lee?" Beth asked anxiously.

Stan folded her in his arms. For a long moment he said nothing as he held her close. At last he spoke.

"He is going to be all right." He drew a deep breath of relief. "He stopped breathing once, but his heart started to beat again and breathing continued. He is coming along fine now."

"Where is George?" I asked.

"He is talking to Dr. Matthews," Stan answered. "A nurse brought him into the operating room."

Together the three of us walked down the hall, into the elevator and to the outside of the building. Stan took Beth's arm and grasping mine firmly, led us around the hospital until we faced the east. We stood facing the morning light. Streaks of coral stretched across the sky, a bright glow of light outlining the horizon. Stan stood tall and calm as he looked into the dawn. His face was granite, his mouth firm and a light glowed in his eyes. Quietly we three stood together, Beth and I watching this man who was with us, yet was far beyond us. After awhile he turned and placed his hands on my shoulders.

"Aunt Gen," he said steadily, "Jesus *is* a living reality." The words were positive pronouncement. They left no room for doubt or denial.

I looked into Stan's face. Light seemed to glow upon it and strength to flow from his hands.

"When I knew that I had to have Him, then Jesus was with me. He rode in that ambulance too. I know it! He filled me with strength and made me greater than myself. If Lee had died I'd have known that the living Christ was there just the same."

Stan's voice had a vibrant quality. He dropped his hands from my shoulders and turned again to face the rising sun. So he stood, looking full into the morning. A new day was dawning for this young man and for his ministry.

I thought of another, unsure of himself, who met the Master on a lake shore one morning long ago. Jesus knew his man, for while Peter was yet vacillating, Jesus called him a Rock. Now, another man who would follow Christ had found him to be the living Lord and had found within himself the steadfastness of a rock.

THE END

BOOKS BY GENEVIEVE PARKHURST
Healing The Whole Person
Healing And Wholeness
Take A Walk With Jesus